# DUCT TAPE ENGINEER

# THE BOOK OF
# **BIG, BIGGER, AND EPIC**
# DUCT TAPE PROJECTS

# DUCT TAPE ENGINEER

## FROM BACKPACKS TO KAYAKS, WRITING DESKS TO ROCKET LAUNCHERS

ROCKPORT

Quarto is the authority on a wide range of topics.

Quarto educates, entertains and enriches the lives of our readers—enthusiasts and lovers of hands-on living.

www.QuartoKnows.com

First published in the United States
of America in 2017 by
Rockport Publishers, an Imprint of
Quarto Publishing Group USA Inc.
100 Cummings Center
Suite 406-L
Beverly, Massachusetts 01915-6101
Telephone: (978) 282-9590
Fax: (978) 283-2742
QuartoKnows.com
Visit our blogs at QuartoKnows.com

10 9 8 7 6 5 4 3 2 1

ISBN: 978-1-63159-130-3

Digital edition published in 2017.

Library Of Congress
Cataloging-In-Publication Data

Names: Akiyama, Lance, author.
Title: Duct Tape Engineer : The Book of Big,
Bigger, and Epic Duct Tape
   Projects / Lance Akiyama.
Description: Beverly, Massachusetts : Rockport
Publishers, [2017]
Identifiers: Lccn 2016032103 | Isbn
9781631591303 (Softbound)
Subjects: Lcsh: Tape Craft. | Duct Tape.
Classification: Lcc Tt869.7 .A45 2017 | Ddc 745.5-
-Dc23
Lc Record Available At Https://Lccn.loc.
gov/2016032103

Photography: Kaile Akiyama
Illustrations: Ali Phelps
Cover and layout: Timothy Samara

Printed in China

**DEDICATION**
For my endlessly supportive friends,
family, and colleagues who cheer
on my eccentric career. You make me
believe that building things out of
cardboard and sticks is a legitimate
job; and to those close to home, who
happily tolerate half of the house
being filled with cardboard furniture.

# CONTENTS

# BIG
# BIGGER
# AND EPIC

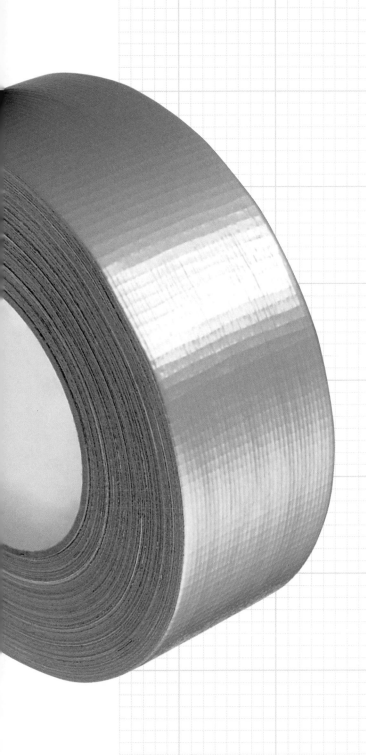

## INTRODUCTION

Roll up your sleeves, declutter the workbench, and stake out a space in the garage. You're going to need it—or perhaps the whole backyard—when you become a duct tape engineer.

The fourteen projects in this book range in size from backpacks to kayaks, from writing desks to rocket launchers. We'll show you how to make a geodesic dome that you can use as a greenhouse, a sturdy toolbox, a catapult, and a queen-size bed frame, as well as all of the rest of the bedroom furniture in case you can't stop taping once you get started.

If you've never worked with duct tape before, don't worry. We've demystified the basic techniques in chapter 1. After that, every project is shown with step-by-step directions.

Bigger doesn't necessarily mean harder—just more fun. All you need is time, determination, and duct tape. Lots and lots of duct tape.

LANCE AKIYAMA

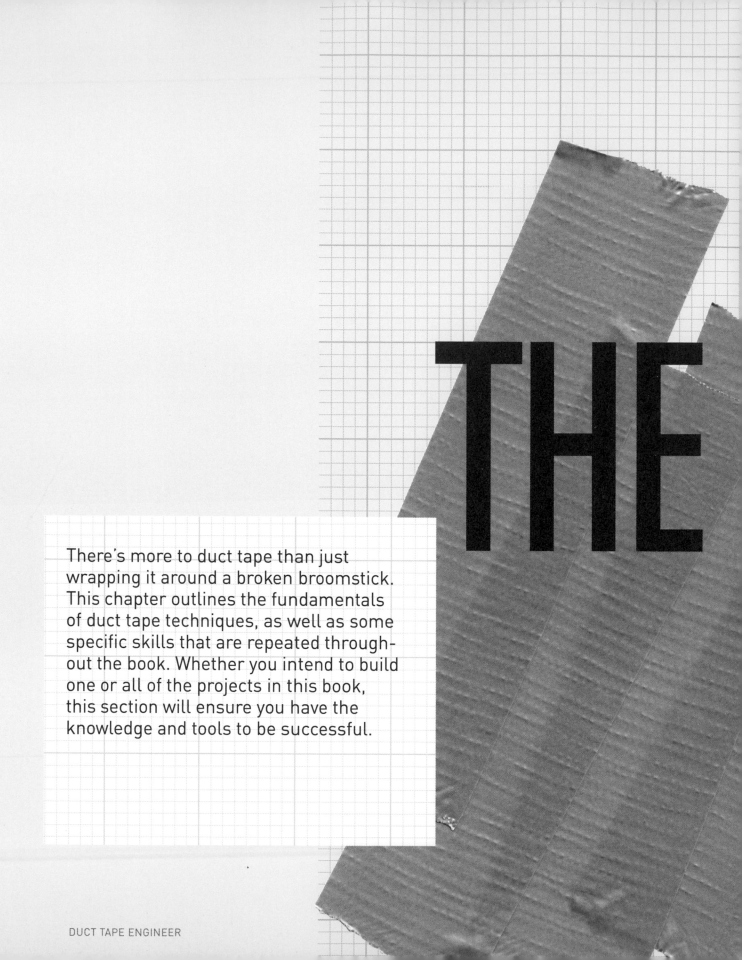

# THE

There's more to duct tape than just wrapping it around a broken broomstick. This chapter outlines the fundamentals of duct tape techniques, as well as some specific skills that are repeated throughout the book. Whether you intend to build one or all of the projects in this book, this section will ensure you have the knowledge and tools to be successful.

# BASICS

# RIPPING
# AND
# CUTTING

The quickest, easiest, and best way to divide a strip of duct tape is to rip it. Duct tape is designed to be torn easily. Pinch the tape with both hands and rip the tape a little. Once the tape begins ripping, it'll be easy to tear the whole piece.

To trim duct tape, it's best to use a rotary cutter. The adhesive gums up scissors blades, making them difficult to use. If you must use scissors to cut detailed shapes, purchase an inexpensive pair and clean the blades with rubbing alcohol after each use.

### THE RIGHT TAPE FOR THE JOB

There is a lot of variation in duct tapes, both in quality and intended function. The original duct tape was made of cotton "duck" canvas, embedded with glue. The woven base gave it its strength and flexibility. Duct tapes today range from styles specially designed for outdoor conditions, tapes designed to be weight bearing, and colorful patterned tapes that are great for lighter jobs and decorative finishes.

For each project, I specify the type of tape and include a list of the actual tapes used. For your safety, and for the success of your project, *please use the recommended type*.

If the duct tape you have on hand is paper thin with few fibers, or if it doesn't rip cleanly, then it's useful only for light duty or decorative work. Except for the projects in chapter 3, I strongly recommend using heavy-duty duct tape—Duck® brand's Max Strength DuckTape® is usually sufficient. ShurTech® brand's T-Rex Tape® is even more durable.

# RECOMMENDED TOOLS

Many of the projects in this book use a basic set of tools. If you intend to become a true duct tape engineer, I suggest having these tools on hand.

CUTTING MAT

MEASURING TAPE AND/OR
METAL RULER

ROTARY CUTTER

UTILITY KNIFE

INEXPENSIVE SCISSORS

DRY CLOTH

GARDEN SAW
FOR CUTTING BAMBOO

PVC PIPE CUTTERS

HOT GLUE GUN

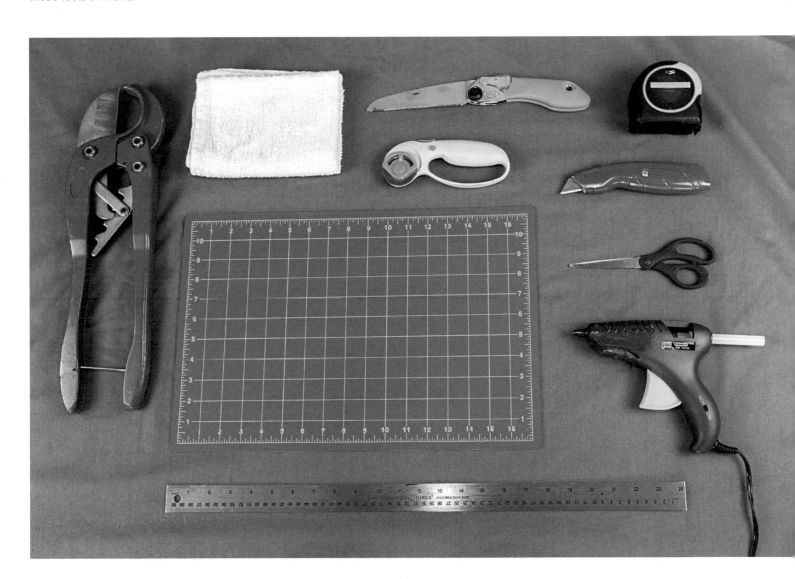

# TAPING TECHNIQUES

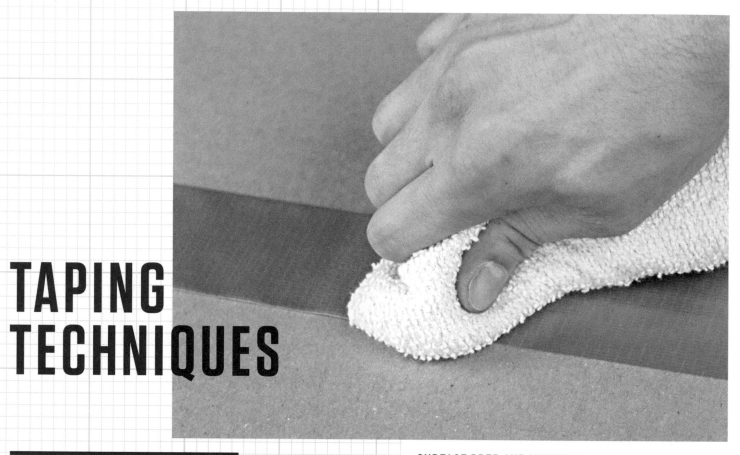

There's more to applying duct tape than just slapping it on. Anything that comes between the adhesive and the surface will make the bond weaker. Read on for tips to ensure your tape does the job.

### SURFACE PREP AND MAXIMUM ADHESION

It's crucial to clean surfaces of dust, oil, and moisture before taping. Wiping surfaces clean with a dry cloth is usually sufficient. If not, wash with soap and let dry.

For maximum adhesion, press the tape firmly onto the surface. Duct tape is a pressure-sensitive adhesive. The adhesive on duct tape works by penetrating the pores of the surface it's on. Therefore, the more pressure you apply, the better it sticks.

To apply even pressure along a long piece of tape, grip a dry cloth in your hand, press it on the tape, and slide it along the tape's backing.

## CROSS TAPING

Duct tape has a high tensile strength, which means it can withstand a lot of force pulling on it. (We've all seen the picture of a car suspended in the air with duct tape!) However, duct tape can usually be peeled away from a surface with much less force. To prevent tape from peeling, place a second piece of tape perpendicular to the first, forming a cross.

## CORNERING AND CURVING

Flat tape does not fit over corners or curves very well. However, you can neatly apply tape to curves by slitting it with a utility knife. Fold the two tape halves over each other, as shown.

### NOTE

Duct tape doesn't stick well to textured surfaces, such as concrete, certain kinds of fabric, or anything that's even slightly wet. Instead, choose a nonstick surface such as plywood or plastic. Experiment to find out which surfaces allow tape to adhere slightly but also easily peel away.

## MINIMIZING IMPERFECTION

When duct tape sticks to itself, it's practically impossible to unstick. Save yourself a lot of aggravation by discarding lengths of tape that are stuck to each other. For wrinkles in tape you've already applied, smooth them out by pressing a dry cloth on the wrinkles.

# HOW TO MAKE A DUCT TAPE SHEET

**1** Choose a nonstick surface (see note on page 15) for your work area. Overlap pieces of tape in the length desired directly onto the work surface. Each new piece of tape applied should cover half the width of the previous piece. Keep the tape taut as you lay it down, and use your free hand to smooth it into place. Press down on each piece to remove air bubbles and ensure that the tape adheres completely.

**2** Pull up the sheet, starting with the first layer. **If you start with the final layer, you may accidentally tear the sheet in half.**

**A large sheet of duct tape is ideal for any project that uses the tape as a fabric or requires an expansive surface. Creating a large sheet that you can then cut into smaller pieces minimizes imperfections and gives your projects a clean, uniform finish. It also makes building a large project more enjoyable: Once the sheet is done, you can focus on assembling your creation quickly.**

**This sheet is double sided, making it extremely strong and durable. Create a reversible sheet with two colors, as in this example, or have fun with a striped sheet by alternating colors when you apply each new row of tape. Here are the steps to creating a perfect duct tape sheet.**

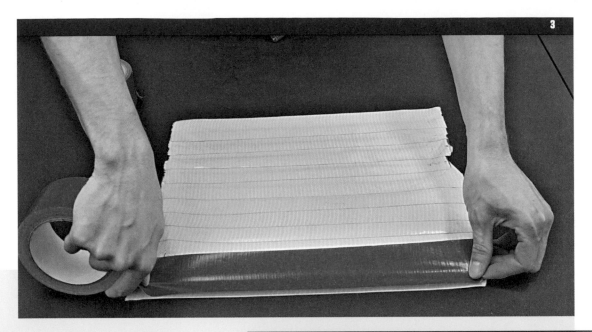

**3** Flip the sheet over, tape it in place so it doesn't shift, and finish the reverse side in the same way as the first. Work slowly and deliberately: It's difficult to adjust a long piece of tape once the two adhesive surfaces are stuck together. If a mistake occurs, smooth it out as best as you can, and consider applying another layer of tape to cover the imperfections.

**4** Trim the uneven edges with a rotary cutter.

**5** You're finished! Take a moment to bask in satisfaction—it is quite gratifying.

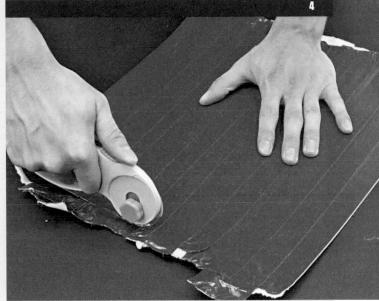

*Our DUCK TAPE SHEET uses* **Duck**® *brand's* **Color Duck Tape**® *in red and blue.*

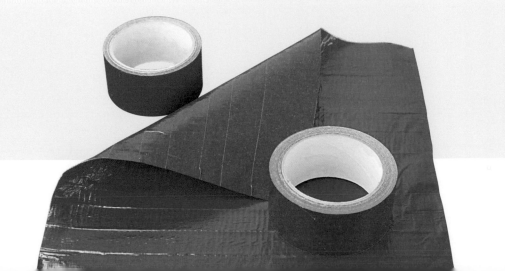

# 1

# FUR

Make an entire bedroom suite from duct tape and cardboard? Most definitely! In these pages, you'll discover how to construct a desk, a chair, a tall dresser, and a queen-size bed frame using your two favorite building supplies and ordinary hardware. These pieces are good looking and sturdy—designed to hold up to regular use over a long period of time. Best of all, you can customize the sizes to fit any dorm or den, waterproof the surfaces, and decorate them with duct tape colors and prints.

**CHOOSE YOUR CARDBOARD WISELY.**

Each piece of furniture in this chapter is weight bearing, to some degree. Make sure the corrugated cardboard you use is structurally sound; avoid any pieces that are crushed, torn, or water damaged.

I used large, double-thick cardboard moving boxes for each project here. Double-thick cardboard provides twice the load-bearing strength of ordinary mailing boxes and is far more resistant to dents and other damage. You can buy oversized double-thick boxes at hardware stores, moving supply stores, and online. Shop around before you buy, as prices can vary widely.

# NITURE

No carpentry skills required. This chair is lightweight, durable, and as strong as any chair made of wood. Its simple geometric shapes and construction techniques make it the perfect starter project for your exploration of duct tape furniture.

# DESK CHAIR

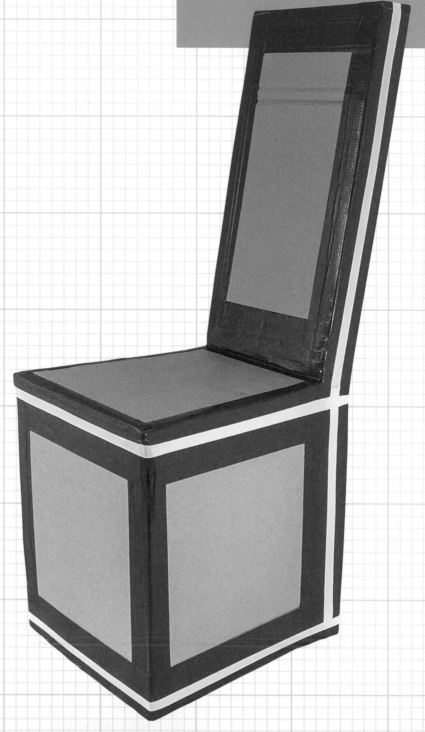

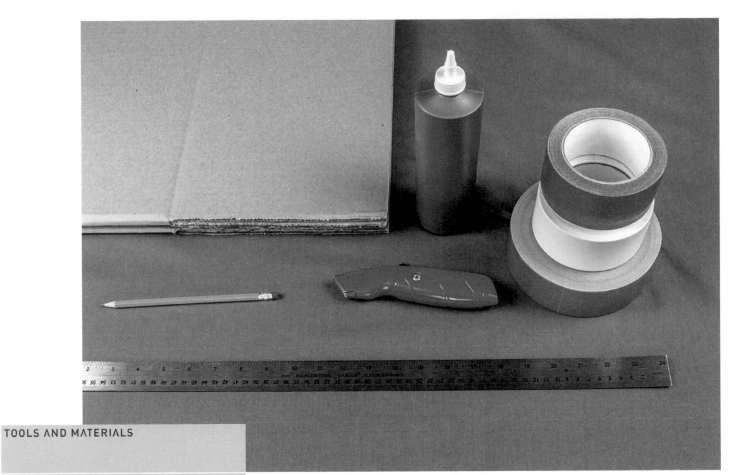

## TOOLS AND MATERIALS

**5 PIECES HEAVY-DUTY DOUBLE-THICK CARDBOARD BOXES, 18" × 18" × 24" (45.5 × 45.5 × 61 CM)**

**METAL RULER**

**UTILITY KNIFE**

**PENCIL**

**30 YARDS (27.5 M) HEAVY-DUTY DUCT TAPE**

**ALL-PURPOSE WHITE GLUE**

**HEAVY OBJECTS FOR WEIGHTS**

**25 YARDS (23 M) COLORED TAPE (OPTIONAL)**

### USE A STRAIGHTEDGE

This project requires precision cuts and straight lines. Use a straightedge at every step to ensure your lines and cuts are straight and accurate.

**1** To make the seat, first decide on the size. Measure and cut four seat pieces, all the same size. I've modeled my chair seat on the dimensions of an actual dining chair: narrower at the back, wider in the front. A square seat or any geometric shape that is at least 12" (30.5 cm) per side would work just as well.

**2** Stack three of the seat pieces (the fourth piece will be used on the bottom of the chair). Tape them together along each of the four sides. This creates a thick seat that resists wear.

**3** To make the base, first decide on the height: The seats of most chairs are about 19" (48.5 cm) high. Make sure all of the corrugations for the base run from top to bottom. This adds significant strength to the chair's structure.

Cut four pieces of cardboard, each the same height. Tape the four pieces of cardboard together to create a box without a top or bottom that precisely fits within the outline of your chair seat. Be sure each piece is the same width as the seat's edges. Then trim the width of two side pieces so the seat will fit on top of the box without falling in. Place the seat squarely on top of the box and tape it in place along all four edges.

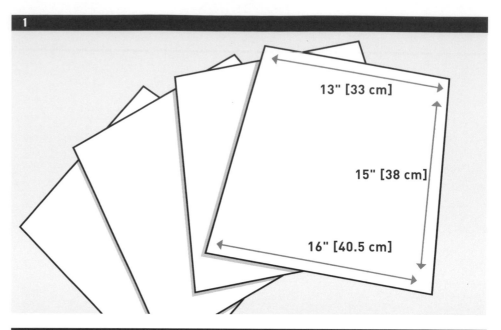

13" [33 cm]

15" [38 cm]

16" [40.5 cm]

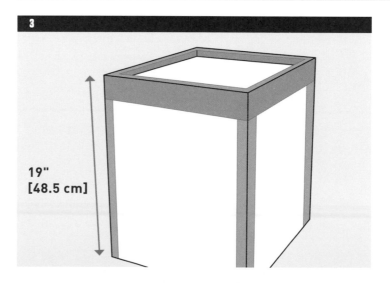

19" [48.5 cm]

**4** To create the internal supports, turn the base upside down and measure the distance between the front and back. Measure and cut two identical rectangles, the same height as the base, that fit snugly between the front and the back. Lay the two rectangles on your work surface. Measure and cut two ¼" (0.6 cm)-wide slits in each. Make the slits evenly spaced, about 4" (10 cm) in from the sides, and about half the depth of the base.

With the slits facing up, slip the rectangles into the base and tape the edges to the box, evenly spaced apart from each other and the sides of the base.

**5** Cut two more rectangles the same height as the sides of the chair. These cross pieces fit into the slits in the first set of supports. Measure the distance between the sides of the base above the slits. (If the seat is tapered, these will not be identical.) Cut the two new rectangles to fit snugly between the sides. Slip the rectangles into the slits for positioning and mark the positions with a pencil.

**6** Place the two new rectangular pieces on your work surface. Cut two ¼" (0.6 cm) slits in each along the pencil marks that you made in step 5. Make the slits half the height of the new pieces. Insert the new rectangles into the first set, fitting the slits together. Apply multiple 4" (10 cm) pieces of tape around all of the intersections in the supports. Apply 6" to 8" (15 to 20.5 cm) pieces of tape to the inside of the box where the supports touch the base and the seat.

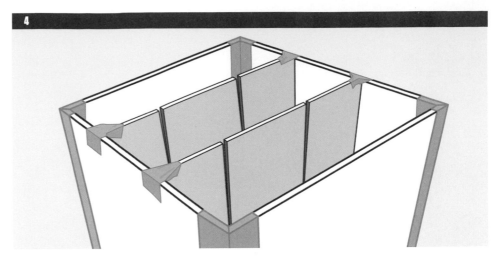

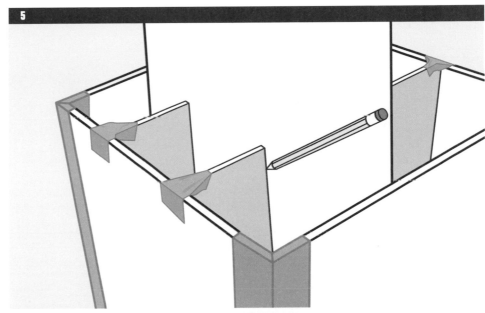

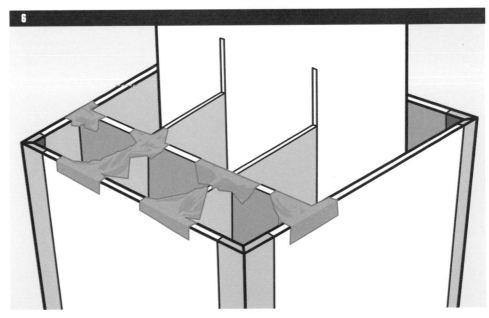

**7_** Tape the fourth seat piece from step 1 to the bottom of the base and turn it right side up. The chair seat is finished! Test it out and while you're sitting there, take a moment to reflect on the path that led you to build a chair out of duct tape and cardboard.

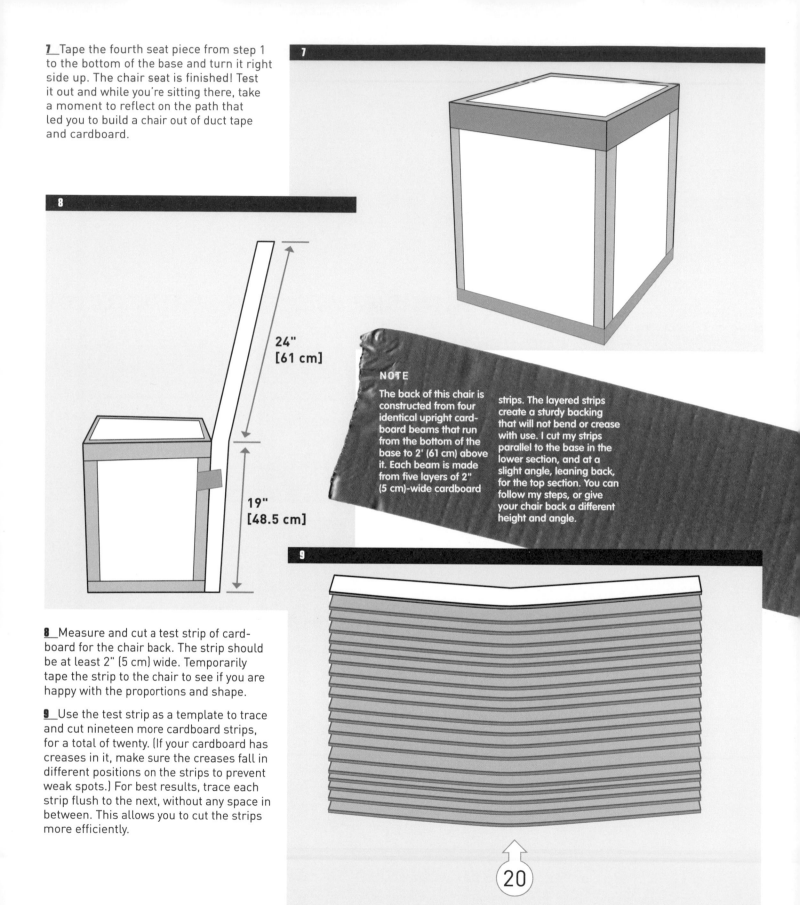

**7**

**8**

24"
[61 cm]

19"
[48.5 cm]

**NOTE**

The back of this chair is constructed from four identical upright cardboard beams that run from the bottom of the base to 2' (61 cm) above it. Each beam is made from five layers of 2" (5 cm)-wide cardboard strips. The layered strips create a sturdy backing that will not bend or crease with use. I cut my strips parallel to the base in the lower section, and at a slight angle, leaning back, for the top section. You can follow my steps, or give your chair back a different height and angle.

**9**

20

**8_** Measure and cut a test strip of cardboard for the chair back. The strip should be at least 2" (5 cm) wide. Temporarily tape the strip to the chair to see if you are happy with the proportions and shape.

**9_** Use the test strip as a template to trace and cut nineteen more cardboard strips, for a total of twenty. (If your cardboard has creases in it, make sure the creases fall in different positions on the strips to prevent weak spots.) For best results, trace each strip flush to the next, without any space in between. This allows you to cut the strips more efficiently.

**10** Stack five strips and wrap them at regular intervals with duct tape to construct the first beam. Do the same three more times.

**11** Make the covering for the beams. Cut a long piece of cardboard that is as wide as the back of the chair, and about 4" (10 cm) longer than two times the length of the beams. (You may need to tape two pieces of cardboard together if you have a tall chair.) Make sure the corrugations are running crosswise to make it easier to fold in the next steps.

Lay the long piece of cardboard on the floor or your work surface. Position the beams on the cardboard: two should be flush with the outer edges of the cardboard, the other two evenly spaced in between. All should line up with the bottom edge of the cardboard. Secure the beams with 10" to 12" (25.5 to 30.5 cm) pieces of tape at the top and bottom.

**12** Cut small strips of cardboard that fit securely between the beams. Fold the strips into triangles and tape them between the beams in several places. These prevent the beams from shifting over time.

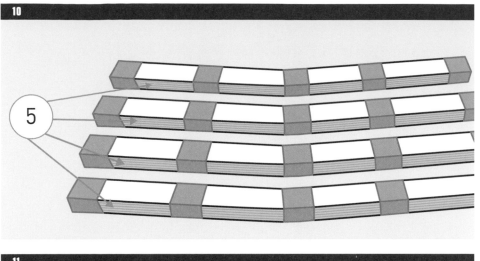

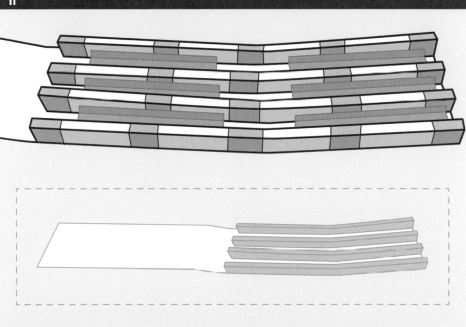

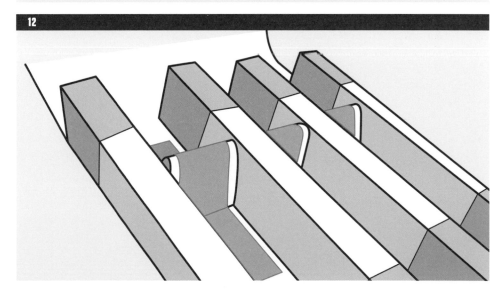

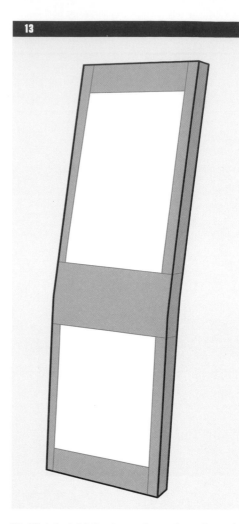

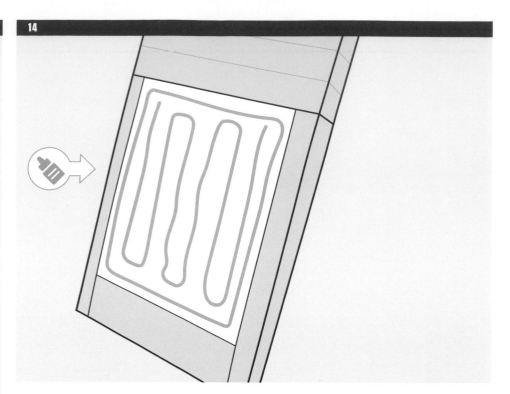

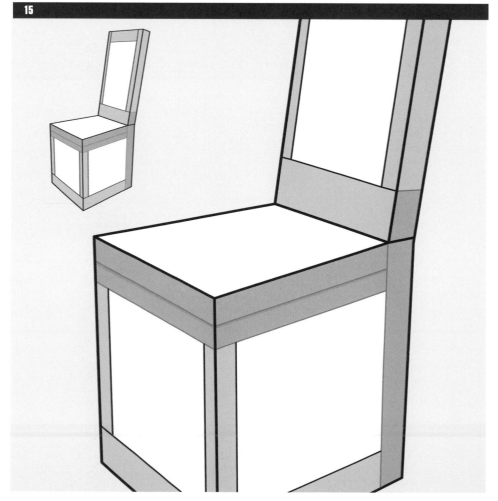

**13** Tightly fold the long piece of cardboard over the top of the beams and along the front. Tape all the seams securely. Wrap tape tightly around the section where the chair back is angled.

**14** Liberally apply all-purpose glue to the chair back, where it will come into contact with the base.

**15** Position the chair back onto the back of the base and firmly press it in place for a tight bond. Wrap duct tape around the top of the base and chair back several times. Tape the seams between the chair back and the seat, as well.

**16** Turn the chair onto its front and place weights on the back to ensure the glue bonds securely. Wait for the glue to dry thoroughly. You're done!

**NOW GET TINKERING!**

This chair is sturdy, but minimal. Consider how you might customize yours. Add armrests, incorporate storage into the seat, add magazine pockets to the sides, or turn it into a throne with a tall, decorative back. Cover the whole chair in tape for added durability and waterproofing. Make it your own!

# DESK

Create the perfect complement to your duct tape chair with a full-size writing desk, complete with a cubby, two sliding drawers, and a load-bearing desktop. This design is as sturdy as any you could buy, and you can customize all the features to meet your productivity needs. Oh, and don't worry, the desk is coffee-spill resistant.

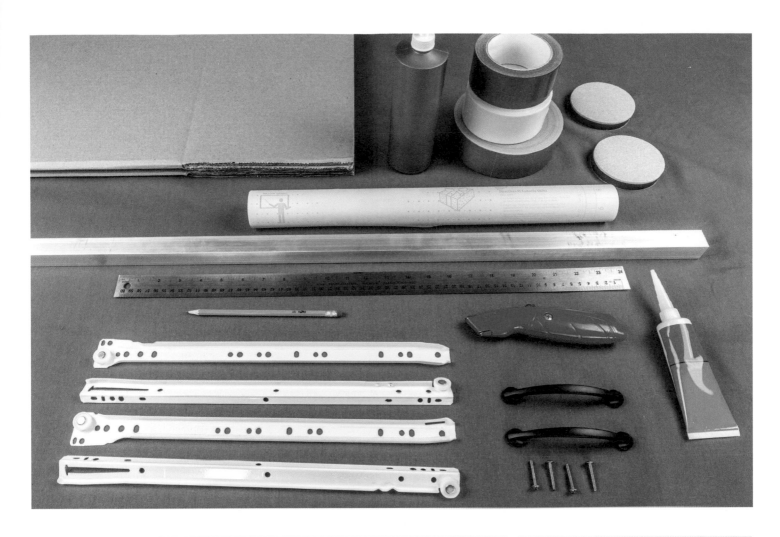

## TOOLS AND MATERIALS

7 HEAVY-DUTY DOUBLE-THICK CARDBOARD BOXES, 18" × 18" × 24" (45.5 × 45.5 × 61 CM)

METAL RULER

UTILITY KNIFE

90 YARDS (82 M) HEAVY-DUTY DUCT TAPE

ALL-PURPOSE GLUE

WEIGHTS

2 SQUARE ALUMINUM RODS, 1" (2.5 CM) WIDE AND 48" (122 CM) LONG

2 SETS 16" (40.5 CM) DRAWER SLIDER HARDWARE

METAL-BONDING GLUE (SUCH AS LIQUID NAILS CONSTRUCTIVE ADHESIVE)

2 DRAWER HANDLES

EXTRA WASHERS AND NUTS THAT FIT THE BOLTS IN THE DRAWER HARDWARE KIT (OPTIONAL)

6 ADHESIVE FURNITURE SLIDERS

8 SQ FT (2.4 SQ M) ADHESIVE PLASTIC LAMINATE

20 YARDS (18 M) COLORED DUCT TAPE (OPTIONAL)

## MATERIAL SUBSTITUTIONS

You can use hot glue instead of all-purpose white glue.

Drawer slider hardware: Forgo the sliders and create a shelf that the drawer sits on. It won't slide as smoothly, but it'll work.

Instead of using the adhesive plastic laminate, cover the desktop entirely in duct tape.

*This project uses **Duck®** brand's **Max Strength Duck Tape®** for the desk construction, **Duck®** brand's **Peel & Stick®** Adhesive Laminate to protect the desktop, and **Duck®** brand's **Color Duck Tape®** in blue and white for decoration.*

**1** Make the supports. The desk's three upright supports are 29" (73.5 cm) high, 2½" (6.5 cm) wide, and 24" (61 cm) deep. Each is constructed from one of the cardboard boxes that's been opened and flattened.

Cut each flattened box to 29" × 53" (73.5 × 134.5 cm). The corrugations should run top to bottom along the 29" (73.5 cm) height.

Measure and crease the cardboard for the four sides of each support. Cut two 2½" × 24" (6.5 × 61 cm) rectangles for the top and bottom, and tape them into place.

**2** Make the back of the desk. Open and flatten a box to double thickness. Lay it on your work surface. Using a metal ruler and utility knife, cut through both thicknesses at once to create a back that is 22" × 48" (56 × 122 cm). Attach the two thicknesses by taping the edges with duct tape.

**3** Attach the back to the uprights. Stand the desk supports on their front edges. The outer supports should be placed at the exact width as the desk's back. The middle support is 10" (25.5 cm) from the support on the right. Apply all-purpose glue to the backs of the supports. Measure to make sure the supports are perfectly parallel.

Carefully lay the desk's back on top of the supports. Double-check that the supports are still parallel. Add weights on top of the glued areas to create a firm bond. When the glue has dried, flip the desk assembly upright. Tape the seams between the supports and the back panel.

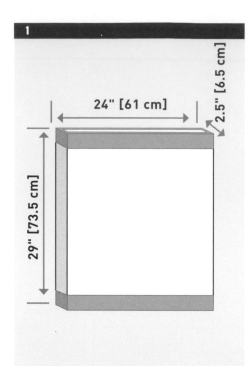

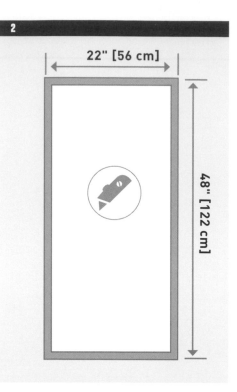

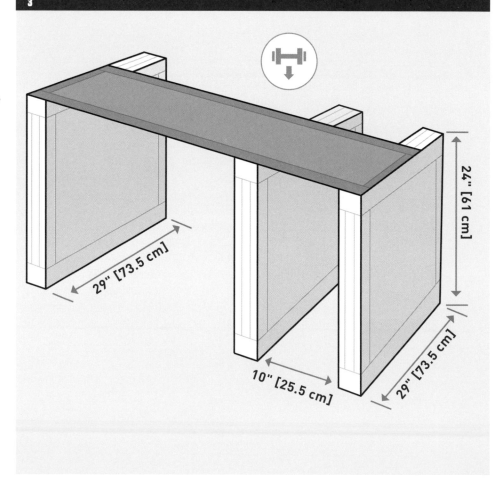

**4** Reinforce the desk top. Cut two slots in the top of each support with a utility knife. Each slot should be 1" (2.5 cm) wide and 1" (2.5 cm) deep. Use the ruler to make sure the slots are aligned with one another across the uprights.

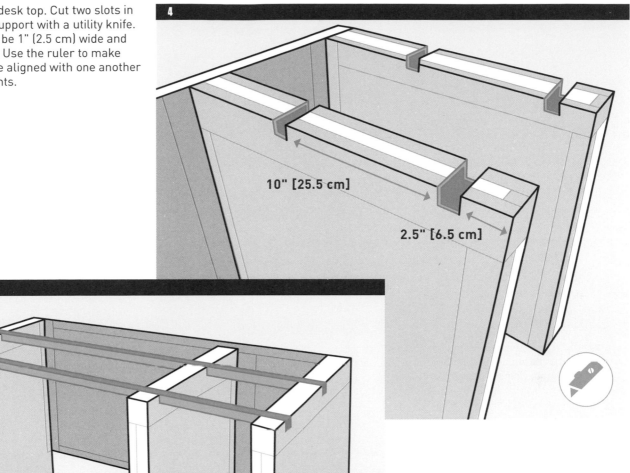

10" [25.5 cm]

2.5" [6.5 cm]

**5** Insert the aluminum rods into the slots. Apply duct tape over the tops to secure them. The rods reinforce the top, ensuring it can hold heavy objects without bending with use.

**6** Measure the dimensions for the desk top. Flatten a heavy-duty cardboard box to double thickness. Transfer the dimensions for the top onto the flattened box and cut through both thicknesses of cardboard. Tape the two layers of cardboard together around all four sides. Attach the top of the desk to the supports with all-purpose glue. Use weights to create a firm bond while the glue is drying. Further secure the desk's top with duct tape around all edges.

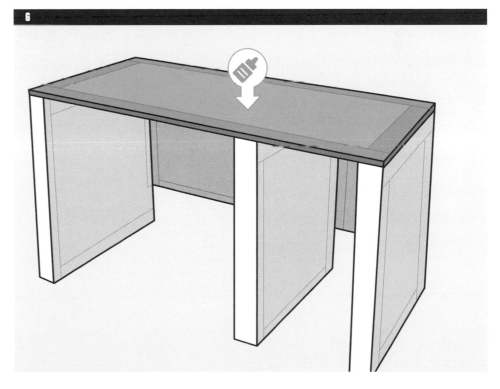

**7** Make the bottom shelf for the desk cubby. Measure the cubby space between the two right-hand supports. Measure and cut a piece of cardboard that fits the interior depth and is about 3" (7.5 cm) wider than the width of the space.

Lay the cardboard rectangle on your work surface. Use a ruler and utility knife to score a groove about 1½" (4 cm) in from each long edge. Fold the edges up and then insert the piece between the two uprights. The goal is to create a shelf, but also to ensure that the space between the two supports is consistent from top to bottom.

**8** Tape the shelf in place on both sides.

**9** Turn the desk upside down. Further secure the shelf by laying duct tape across the underside and the bottoms of the supports. Turn the desk right side up.

**10** Make the top drawer. Cut two 1" × 16" (2.5 × 40.5 cm) strips of cardboard. These support the drawer hardware and must be installed exactly parallel to one another. Measure from the underside of the desk's top to mark the spots for their installation. Hot glue and tape the strips into place. In this example, they are glued 8" (20.5 cm) from the underside of the desktop, and 1" (2.5 cm) from the outside edge of the support.

**11** The drawer hardware is made in two parts. The track is attached to the desk's supports; the glides are attached to the drawer itself. Use metal-bonding glue to attach a track on top of one of the support strips created in step 10. Use small pieces of tape to hold the track in place temporarily while the glue dries. Repeat on the other side.

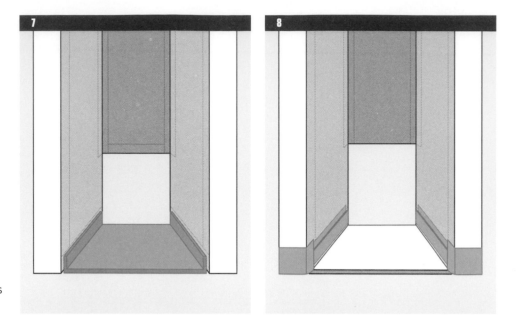

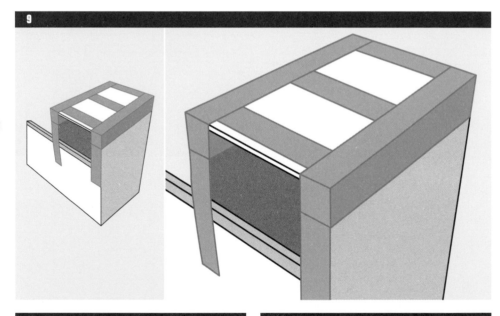

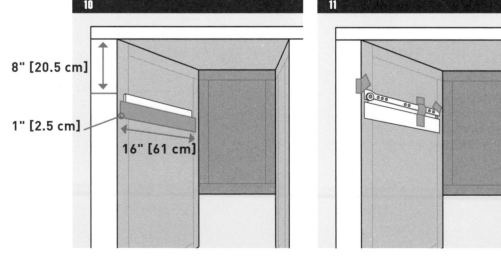

8" [20.5 cm]

1" [2.5 cm]

16" [61 cm]

**12** Measure and cut a piece of cardboard that fits between the two tracks. Test how it fits by holding the glides along the edges of the cardboard and fitting it into the tracks. The drawer should slide smoothly. In this example, the width of the drawer is 1" (2.5 cm) narrower than the space between the uprights; each side of the drawer mechanism takes up ½" (1.3 cm) of space.

**13** Measure the depth of the drawer space, allowing for at least 1" (2.5 cm) of clearance between the top of the drawer and the underside of the desktop. Place the cardboard drawer bottom (without the glides) on your work surface. Cut pieces of cardboard for the front, back, and sides of the drawer. Use hot glue to attach them to the drawer bottom.

**14** Use metal-bonding glue to attach the drawer glides to the bottom edges of the drawer. Use small pieces of tape to hold the glides in place until the glue dries.

## WHY SO MANY KINDS OF GLUE?

White glue, hot glue, and metal-bonding glue all have their best uses and downsides.

All-purpose white glue is cheap, easy to work with, and bonds very well to cardboard. It does not work on nonporous materials, such as metal.

Hot glue also works well with cardboard and is great when you need a quick bond. However, it can be difficult to use when covering a large area because it dries so quickly.

Metal-bonding glue can be used for all applications in this project, but it's expensive and more noxious than either of the other two glues.

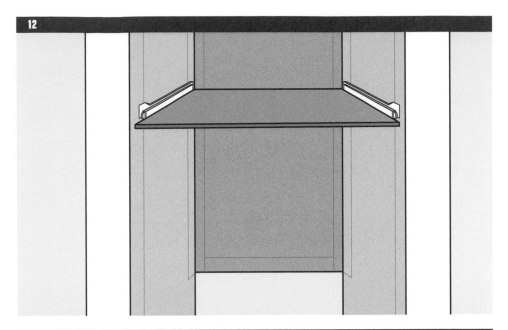

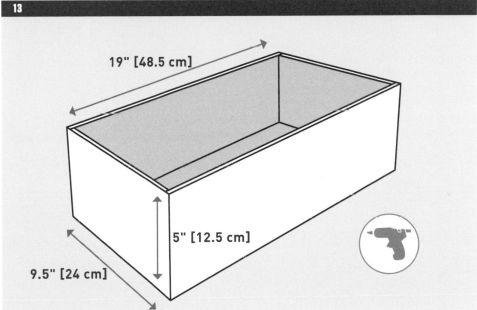

19" [48.5 cm]

5" [12.5 cm]

9.5" [24 cm]

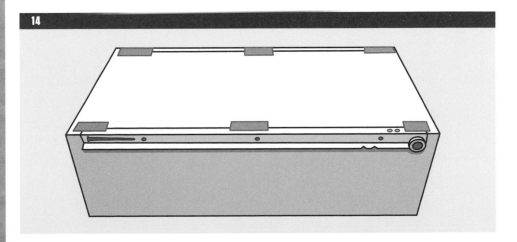

**15** Repeat with a second drawer, or even a third. Always ensure the upright supports are exactly parallel to each other and test fit the bottom of the drawer before assembly.

**16** Fill in the gap between the drawers by hot gluing a small piece of cardboard between the supports and then covering it with duct tape.

**17** Make a façade for the front of each drawer. The façades should be about 3" (7.5 cm) taller and wider than the actual drawer fronts. Attach the façades to the drawers with hot glue, applying pressure for a tight bond.

**18** Install the drawer handles as you would on any other drawer. Add another layer of cardboard inside the drawer front or washers use extra if needed, so the handle screws will be tight.

**19** Turn the desk onto its back and apply six adhesive furniture sliders to the bottom of the desk, two under each support.

**20** Protect the top of the desk from coffee spills by applying a layer of adhesive plastic laminate. Duck® brand offers Peel & Stick Adhesive Laminate in a 20" (51 cm)-wide roll, which is perfect for this desk. Secure the edges of the laminate by applying tape around the perimeter.

**You're done! Now set up your computer and exult in your creation!**

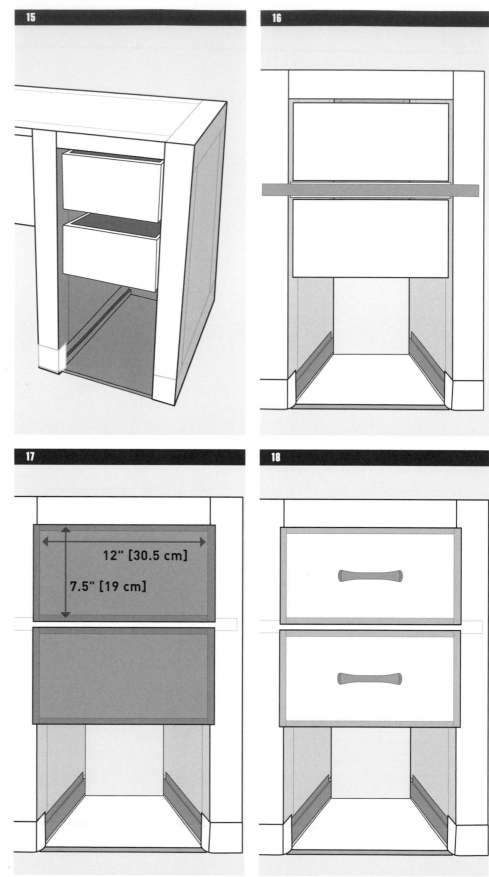

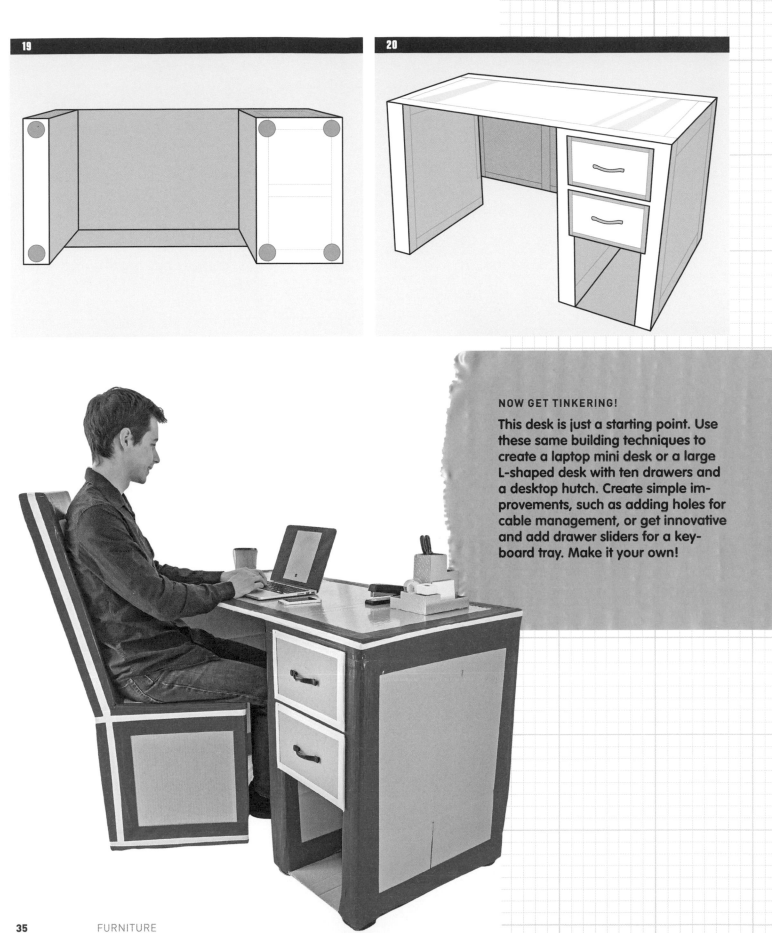

**19**

**20**

## NOW GET TINKERING!

This desk is just a starting point. Use these same building techniques to create a laptop mini desk or a large L-shaped desk with ten drawers and a desktop hutch. Create simple improvements, such as adding holes for cable management, or get innovative and add drawer sliders for a keyboard tray. Make it your own!

Create a full-size dresser with sliding drawers. I'll show you one possible design and then it's up to you to choose how many drawers you want, what sizes they should be, and any other custom features for this epic project.

# DRESSER

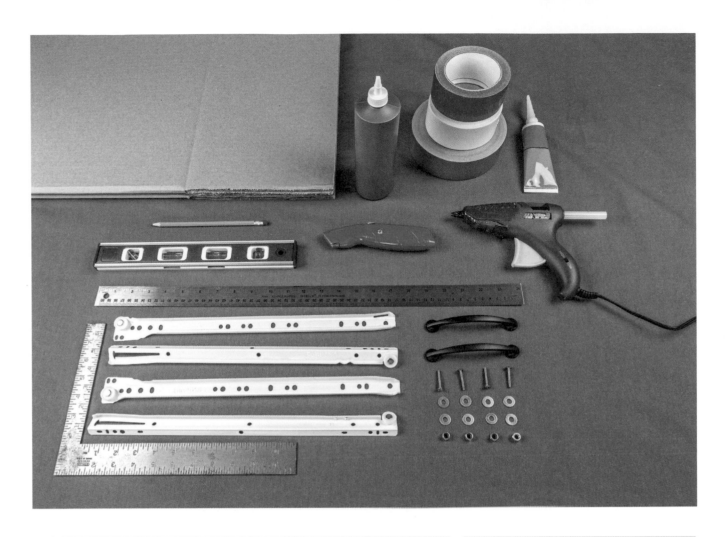

## TOOLS AND MATERIALS

**8 HEAVY-DUTY DOUBLE-THICK
CARDBOARD BOXES, 18" × 18" × 24"
(45.5 × 45.5 × 61 CM)**

**UTILITY KNIFE**

**METAL RULER**

**30 YARDS (27.5 M) HEAVY-DUTY
DUCT TAPE**

**HOT GLUE**

**ALL-PURPOSE WHITE GLUE**

**STEEL SQUARE**

**LEVEL**

**6 SETS DRAWER SLIDER HARDWARE**

**METAL-BONDING GLUE**

**PENCIL**

**10 DRAWER HANDLES**

**EXTRA WASHERS AND NUTS THAT
FIT THE BOLTS IN THE DRAWER
HARDWARE KIT (OPTIONAL)**

**15 YARDS (13.5 M) COLORED
DUCT TAPE (OPTIONAL)**

## MATERIAL SUBSTITUTIONS

You can use any rigid object at least 12" (30.5 cm) square with a 90-degree angle, instead of a steel square.

Drawer slider hardware: Forgo the drawer sliders and, instead, let the drawers rest directly on the shelves. However, without the slider hardware, the drawers will not pull easily. This could cause problems with the drawer fronts pulling loose once the dresser is full of clothes.

*This project uses **Duck®** brand's **Max Strength Duck Tape®** for the dresser construction as well as **Duck®** brand's **Color Duck Tape®** in blue and white for decoration.*

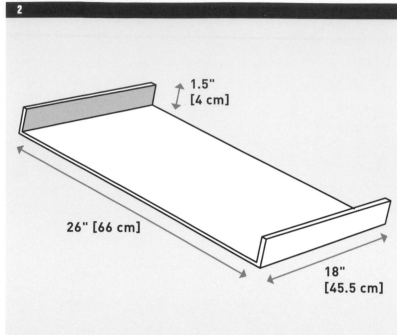

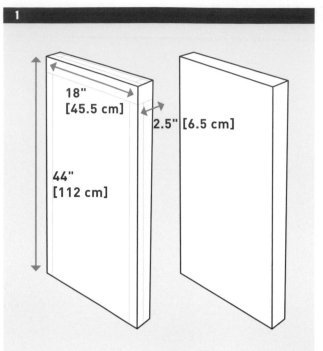

**1** Make the dresser sides. The dresser sides are 44" (112 cm) high, 2½" (6.5 cm) wide, and 18" (45.5 cm) deep. Each is constructed from one of the cardboard boxes that's been opened and flattened. For each side, measure and cut a 41" × 44" (104 × 112 cm) rectangle from the cardboard. Corrugations should run top to bottom along the 44" (112 cm) height.

**2** Make the dresser's top and bottom. Decide on the interior width of the dresser. This example is 26" (66 cm) wide. Cut two identical rectangles equal to the dresser's interior width, plus 3" (7.5 cm). The rectangles used in this example are 29" × 18" (73.5 × 45.5 cm). Score the rectangles 1½" (4 cm) from each edge. Fold the edges as shown to create flaps.

**3** Insert the rectangles from step 2 between the sides of the dresser, with the side flaps facing downward, to create the top and bottom. Use hot glue to adhere the folded flaps in place. Press each flap firmly against the dresser sides while the glue sets. Secure the top and bottom by wrapping the flaps and sides tightly with two layers of duct tape.

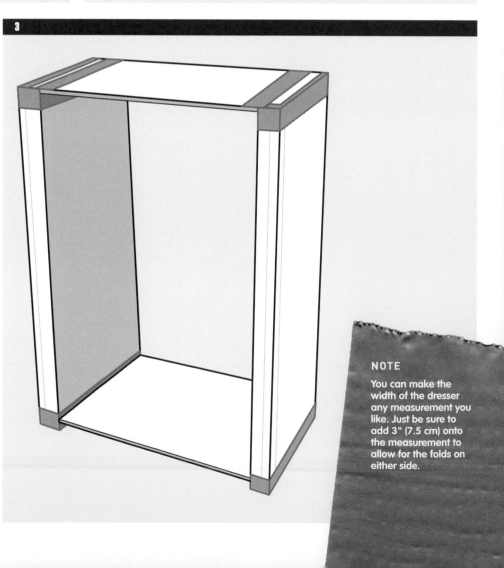

**NOTE**

You can make the width of the dresser any measurement you like. Just be sure to add 3" (7.5 cm) onto the measurement to allow for the folds on either side.

**4**_ Make the dresser's back. Lay the dresser facedown and square the corners using the steel square. Carefully measure the height and width of the dresser. Cut open and flatten one of the boxes. Measure and cut a large rectangle equal to the width and height of the dresser.

Apply all-purpose glue to the back of the side pieces and attach the large rectangle to them. Secure the edges of the rectangle to the sides, top, and bottom of the dresser with tape.

Double-check that the dresser is perfectly square before the glue dries. Allow the glue to dry completely before setting the dresser upright.

**5**_ Make the drawer shelves. Each drawer has a shelf that serves a dual purpose: It supports the drawer slide hardware, and ensures the interior width of the dresser is consistent.

Cut open and flatten one of the boxes. Cut four 29" × 16½" (73.5 × 42 cm) pieces of cardboard for the drawer shelves. Place one of the shelves on your work surface. Measure and score a fold line, 1½" (4 cm) in from each narrow side. Fold the ends at a right angle to the shelf along the scored lines. Repeat with the other three shelves.

**6**_ On the inside of the dresser, carefully measure and mark where the shelves will be placed. Make sure the measurements are parallel on both sides. I've made my top drawer a height of 5½" (14 cm) and the other drawers a height of 8½" (21.5 cm). Make sure the shelves fit by slipping them inside the dresser at the desired positions—they should fit snugly without bending. Make sure all the shelf flaps face upward.

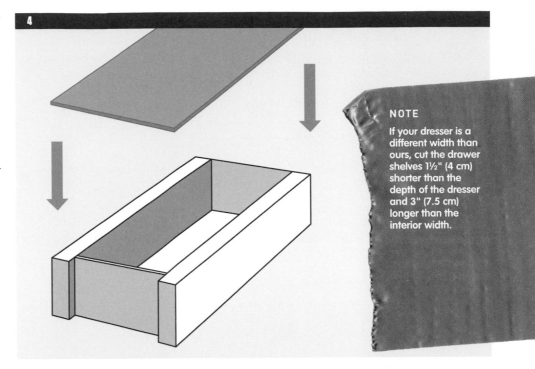

**NOTE**

If your dresser is a different width than ours, cut the drawer shelves 1½" (4 cm) shorter than the depth of the dresser and 3" (7.5 cm) longer than the interior width.

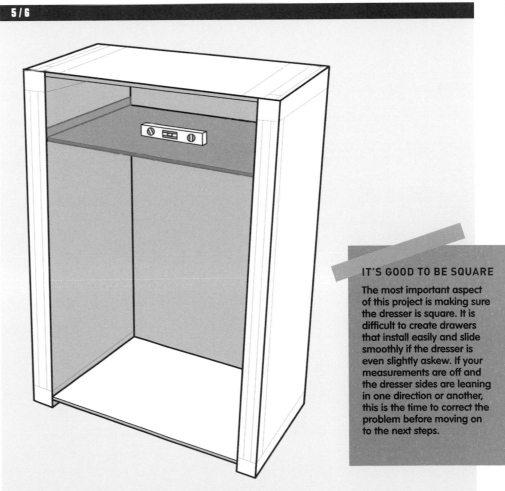

**IT'S GOOD TO BE SQUARE**

The most important aspect of this project is making sure the dresser is square. It is difficult to create drawers that install easily and slide smoothly if the dresser is even slightly askew. If your measurements are off and the dresser sides are leaning in one direction or another, this is the time to correct the problem before moving on to the next steps.

**7** Use a level along the front, back, and sides to ensure that the shelf is perfectly flat and even. Hot glue and then tape the flaps to the inside of the dresser. Double-check that each shelf is level after taping it. Adjust if necessary. Repeat with the other shelves. Allow the glue to dry completely before continuing to the next step.

**8** The drawer hardware is made in two parts. The tracks are attached to the flaps of the dresser shelves. The glides that slide on the track are attached to the drawer bottoms. The bottom edges of the tracks must rest on the shelf to help bear the weight of the drawers. Use metal-bonding glue to attach the tracks to the shelves. Use small pieces of tape to temporarily hold the tracks in place while the glue dries. Repeat on each shelf.

**9** If you are making your dresser with two small drawers on top, as I have done, use hot glue to install a small cardboard divider between the two small drawers. This supports the drawer slider hardware and ensures the shelf doesn't sag.

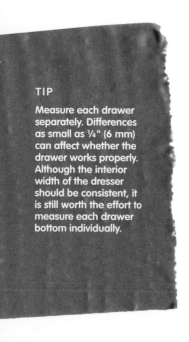

**TIP**

Measure each drawer separately. Differences as small as ¼" (6 mm) can affect whether the drawer works properly. Although the interior width of the dresser should be consistent, it is still worth the effort to measure each drawer bottom individually.

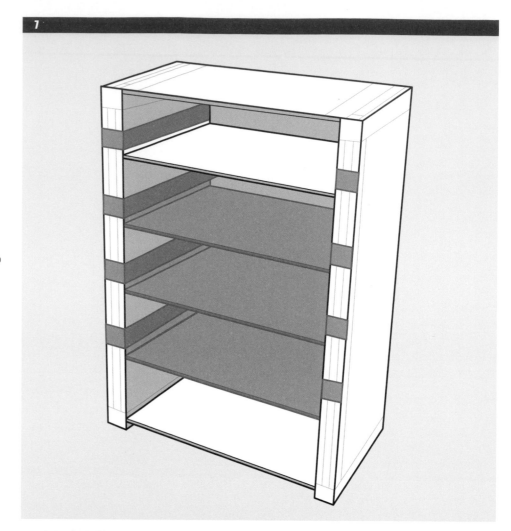

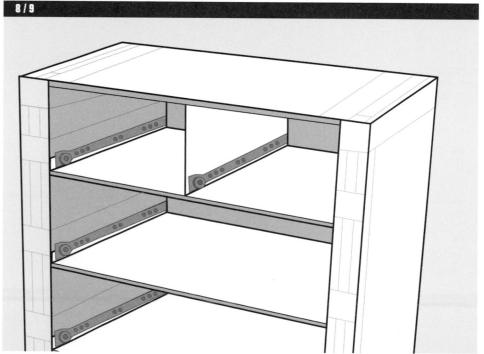

**10** Make the drawers. Start with the drawer bottom. Measure and cut a piece of cardboard that fits between the two bottom tracks and is about 2" (5 cm) shorter than the depth of the dresser. Test how it fits by using your hands to hold the glider along the edges of the drawer bottom and fitting it into the tracks. The drawer should slide smoothly.

**11** Measure the height of the drawer spaces, allowing at least 1½" (4 cm) of clearance between the top of the drawer and the shelf above it. Place a cardboard drawer bottom (without the glides) on your work surface. Cut pieces of cardboard for the front, back, and sides of the drawer. Use hot glue to attach them to the drawer bottom. (Note that the sides should sit on the top of the drawer bottom, not the outer edges, so as not to alter the drawer width.) Repeat for each drawer.

**12** Apply metal-bonding glue to the drawer sliders and then attach them to the bottom edges of the drawers. Use tape to hold the sliders in place until the glue dries completely.

**13** Fit all of the drawers onto the sliders. If you measured each drawer to fit specific shelves, make sure they match up.

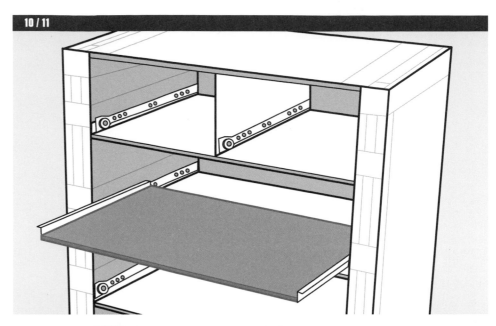

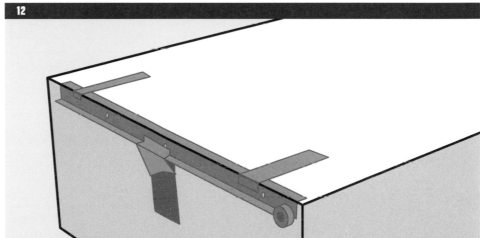

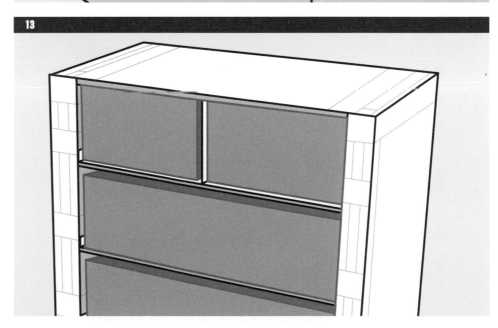

**14** Fill the gaps between the shelves. Cut narrow strips of cardboard the width of the drawers and the depth of the gap. Use hot glue to attach the strips to the shelves and then cover them with duct tape.

**15** Add façades (fronts) to the drawers. Cut cardboard façades that are about 1½" (4 cm) wider and ½" (1.3 cm) deeper than each drawer front. Center and hot glue the façades into place and allow the glue to set.

**16** Install drawer handles on each drawer as you would on any other piece of furniture. For the larger drawers, use two handles per drawer. Use both when pulling the drawer open. If necessary, insert an extra layer of cardboard inside the drawer fronts or use extra washers to ensure that the drawer handle screws attach firmly.

**17** Finish by gluing a double-thick rectangle of cardboard on the dresser top. The rectangle should overhang the right and left sides by about 1" (2.5 cm). Cover the edges with tape. Enjoy your duct tape dresser that functions as well as it looks!

**NOTE**
If you wish to cover the edges of the façades with decorative tape, do so before attaching them to the drawers.

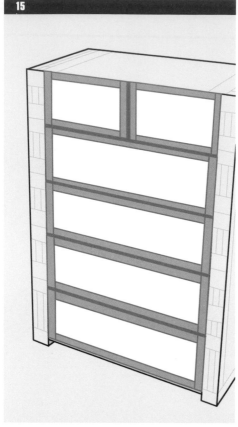

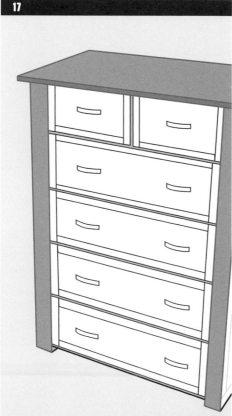

## NOW GET TINKERING!

The techniques in this chapter can be applied to make custom dressers. The size and shape are up to you. However, I don't recommend making drawers wider than 26" (66 cm); the wider the dresser, the harder it is to make sure the interior width is consistent.

Make multiple smaller drawers, or scale down these ideas to create a dresser extension that sits on top of an existing one. Or make a double-wide dresser with an additional upright support between the drawers on either side. Get crafty by adding false backs to the drawers for hidden compartments, or attach hooks on the side to hang your belts and accessories. The best part is making it your own.

Push the limits of duct tape and cardboard construction with your own DIY bed frame. Simple, customized, and lightweight, this frame is perfect for those who don't want to invest in a pricey piece of furniture. The dimensions of this project are for a queen-size bed. For other bed sizes, you can use these same techniques, but make sure the dimensions of the finished pieces will fit your mattress. As far as bedroom furniture goes, it doesn't get any bigger than this—the next step up is to build the bedroom itself!

# BED FRAME

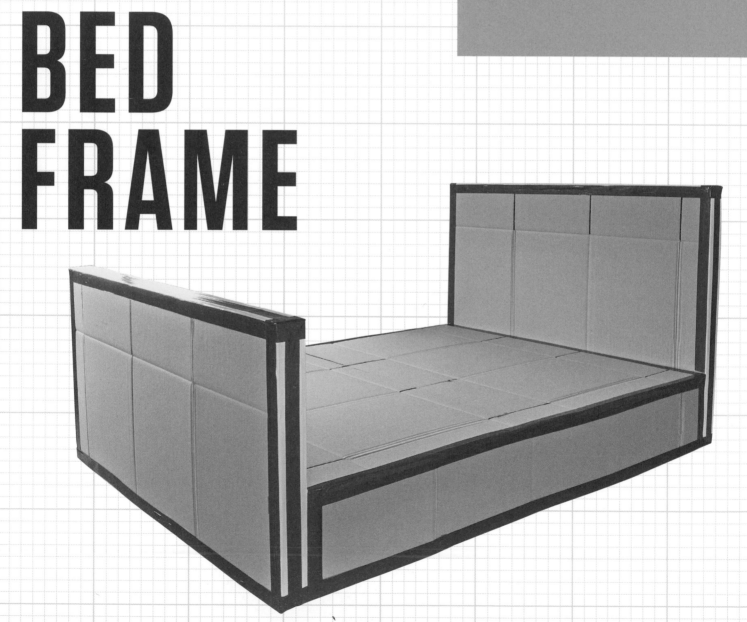

This project uses **Duck®** brand's **Max Strength Duck Tape®** for the bed construction, **Double-Sided Duck® Tape®** for the mattress, and **Color Duck Tape®** in blue and white for decoration.

## TOOLS AND MATERIALS

**22 LARGE HEAVY-DUTY DOUBLE-THICK CARDBOARD BOXES, 18" × 18" × 24" (45.5 × 45.5 × 61 CM)**

**METAL RULER**

**UTILITY KNIFE**

**120 YARDS (110 M) HEAVY-DUTY DUCT TAPE**

**10' (3 M) DOUBLE-SIDED DUCT TAPE**

**35 YARDS (32 M) DECORATIVE TAPE (OPTIONAL)**

## A TIME-INTENSIVE BUILD

Although this project is simple in concept and execution, it requires time and determination to measure and cut all of the bed frame pieces. I strongly recommend sharing the labor with a friend. If you're building solo, turn on some music and settle in for an epic duct tape endeavor.

## BED FRAME PLATFORM

**1**_Make the support structure for the bed. Cut seven 12" × 80" (30.5 × 203.5 cm) cardboard rectangles. You may need to tape two boxes together to achieve the right length.

**2**_Take five of the seven pieces from step 1 and, along one long edge of each, cut seven ¼" (0.6 cm)-wide slots that are 6" (15 cm)-long and spaced 10" (25.5 cm) apart. Set these pieces aside. The other two long pieces from step 1 do not require slots.

**3**_Cut nine 12" × 60" (30.5 × 152.5 cm) cardboard rectangles. Take seven of these and, along one long edge of each, cut five ¼" (0.6 cm)-wide slots that are 6" (15 cm)-long and spaced 10" (25.5 cm) apart. The remaining rectangles do not require slots.

**4**_The 80" (203.5 cm) pieces from step 1 with the slots form the length of the bed. The 60" (152.5 cm) pieces with the slots from step 3 form the width. Fit the pieces together, sliding the slots into one another to create the support structure. This step is incredibly satisfying after all of that cutting! The structure may wobble at this point, but will be stabilized later.

**5**_Create a frame for the bed with the remaining pieces from steps 2 and 3. Tape the sides of the frame together at the corners, covering the sides of the support structure. Apply 8" (20.5 cm) pieces of duct tape to connect the ends of the support pieces to the frame. Firmly pinch the tape over the top edge of each support piece. Flip the bed over and repeat on the other side.

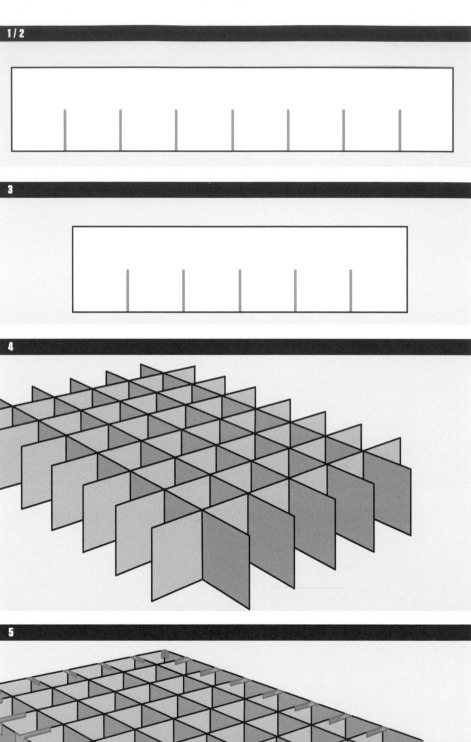

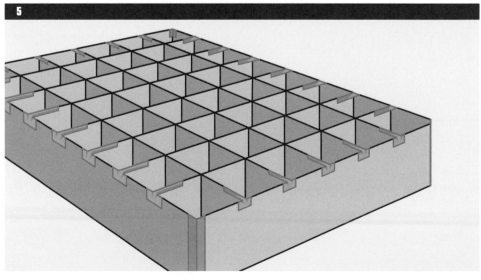

**6** Measure and cut large cardboard pieces to cover the top surface of the bed frame. Firmly apply duct tape around the perimeter, as shown.

The basic bed is finished! You could stop here, however, the next steps transform this cardboard platform to designer status with a headboard and footboard.

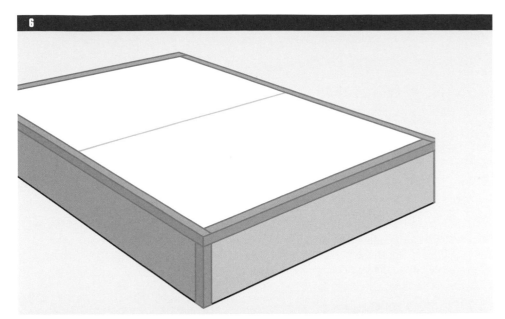

## HEADBOARD AND FOOTBOARD

**1** For the headboard, cut a cardboard rectangle the width of the bed and the height of your choice. My headboard is 43" (109 cm) tall and 60" (152.5 cm) wide.

**2** Cut eleven 3" × 43" (7.5 × 109 cm) strips of cardboard. Tape the strips onto the headboard from step 1, running from top to bottom and spaced 5" (12.5 cm) apart. Place duct tape at the ends of each strip. Firmly pinch the tape over the ends of the strips to ensure a strong bond with the cardboard base.

**3** Cut twelve 9" (23 cm)-long rectangles that are as wide as the space between the headboard support strips. In this example, the width is 4¾" (12 cm). Fold the rectangles in half and then tape the ends into the spaces between the support strips to keep them in place.

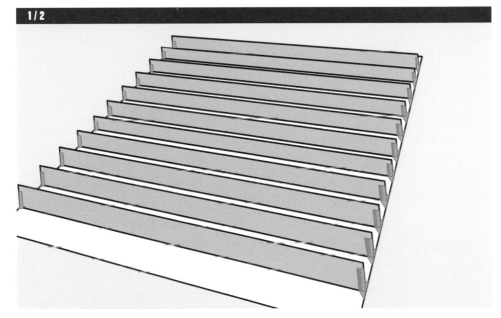

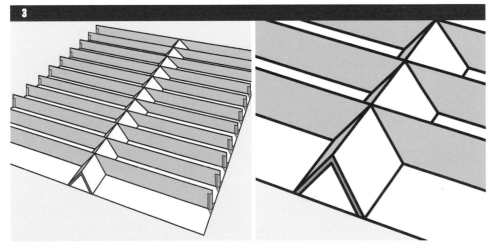

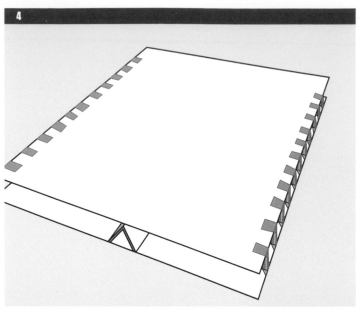

**4**  Attach another 43" × 60" (109 × 152.5 cm) rectangle on top of the existing headboard.

**5**  Cut two 3½" × 43½" (9 × 110.5 cm) rectangles and tape them to the sides of the headboard.

**6**  Cut two 3½" × 80½" (9 × 204.5 cm) rectangles and tape them to the top and bottom of the headboard.

**7**  Wrap long pieces of duct tape around the top and bottom of the headboard as shown. This prevents the first layer of tape from peeling.

**8**  Follow the same process to create a footboard. My example is 30" (76 cm) tall.

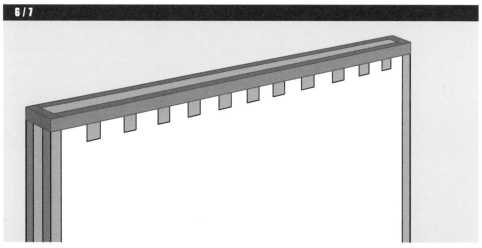

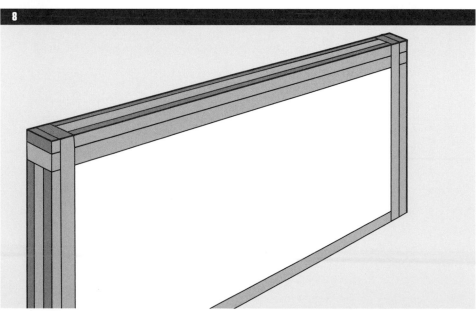

**9** Arrange the bed frame pieces as shown. Apply one piece of duct tape over the seams between the bed platform, headboard, and footboard. Next, apply two 12" (30.5 cm) pieces of tape that connect the bed platform to the headboard and footboard, as shown.

**10** Apply two pieces of double-sided duct tape across the width of the bed frame. This helps prevent the mattress from sliding on the cardboard. The frame is finished!

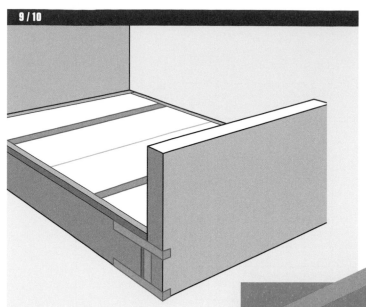

**DESIGN VARIABLES**

After a good night's rest, consider adding small drawers or cubbies to the underside of the bed frame. Build a custom phone-charging mount on the headboard, a built-in night stand, or a place to hang your sleep mask.

# 2

# EVE
# ESS

Everyone can use a new backpack, messenger bag, or toolbox, but the ones you buy might not have all the features you need. In this chapter, I'll show you how to make the basics, along with construction techniques for pockets, straps, and handles. You can modify the size of each project to suit your needs and add as many custom details and compartments as you like. And, of course, make your projects stylish with colored trims and stripes. Your friends will look twice before realizing your everyday essentials are made from duct tape!

These projects are relatively light duty. Feel free to use regular duct tape or colored tape while making the backpack, messenger bag, or toolbox.

# RYDAY
# ENTIALS

51

# BACK-PACK

This duct-tape backpack is durable, inexpensive, and best of all, custom-crafted—just the way you want it. You can create any number of pockets, pouches, secret compartments, and other features. This backpack is also super easy to fix and redesign. Bruise the surface? Patch it with tape! Need more space? Stick on another pocket! These steps will lead you through the basic construction. It's up to you to outfit your pack with personalized features and make it your own.

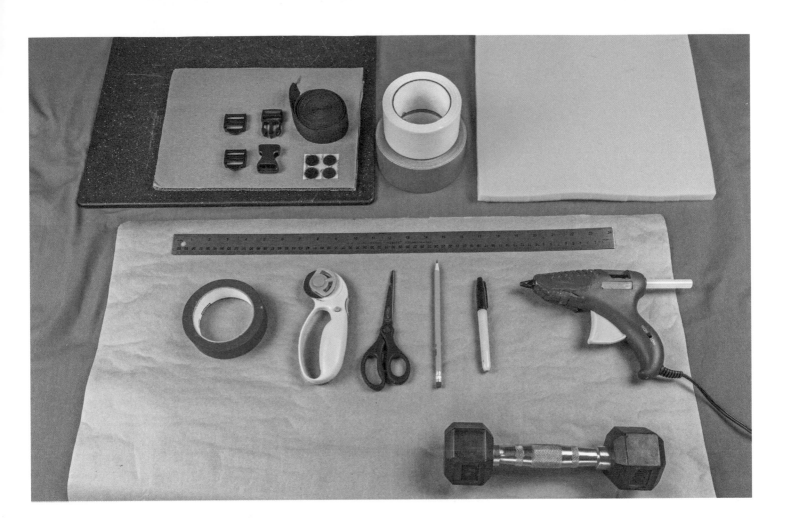

## TOOLS AND MATERIALS

1 LARGE SHEET BROWN PAPER

REMOVABLE TAPE (PAINTER'S TAPE OR MASKING TAPE)

PENCIL

METAL RULER

ROTARY CUTTER OR SCISSORS

90 TO 160 YARDS (82 TO 146 M) MAIN COLOR DUCT TAPE

PERMANENT MARKER

5 YARDS (4.5 M) SECONDARY COLOR DUCT TAPE FOR TRIM

1 SHEET CRAFT UPHOLSTERY FOAM, ½" (1.3 CM) THICK

CORRUGATED CARDBOARD

CUTTING BOARD AND WEIGHTS

3 YARDS (3 M) 1" (2.5 CM)-WIDE NYLON WEBBING

2 PLASTIC STRAP ADJUSTORS (SIZED TO FIT THE 1" (2.5 CM) WEBBING)

1 SIDE RELEASE BUCKLE (SIZED TO FIT THE 1" (2.5 CM) WEBBING)

ADHESIVE-BACKED DOTS (SUCH AS VELCRO)

## MATERIAL SUBSTITUTIONS

You can use newspaper or sheets of paper taped together instead of brown paper.

Any soft, cushiony material can be used in place of craft upholstery foam.

Forgo the webbing, buckles, and adjusters for the straps and simply make them from duct tape. (Note that they won't be adjustable.)

*This project uses **Duck**® brand's **Max Strength Duck Tape**® in silver and **Duck**® brand's **Color Duck Tape**® in yellow.*

**1**

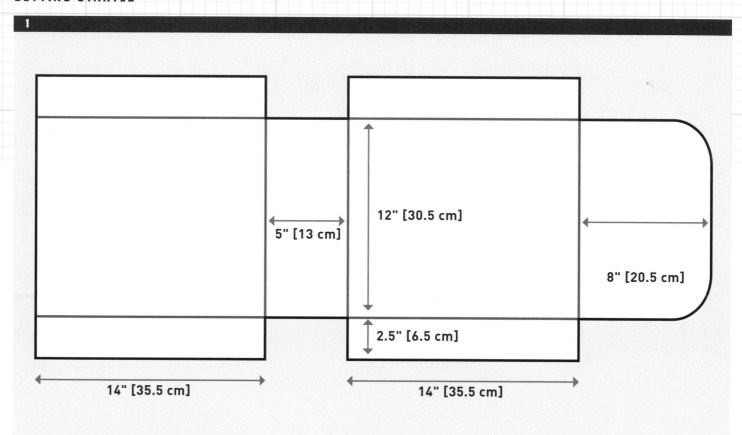

5" [13 cm]

12" [30.5 cm]

8" [20.5 cm]

2.5" [6.5 cm]

14" [35.5 cm]

14" [35.5 cm]

**1**\_Lay the brown paper on your work surface and tape it in place. Draw and then cut out your backpack template to the size you want. Having a template allows you to easily fix mistakes before cutting a large sheet of duct tape. The dimensions shown here are only one option. Customize the backpack to fit your needs.

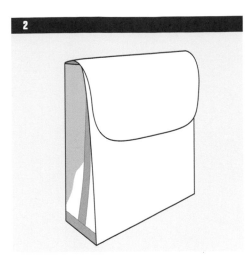

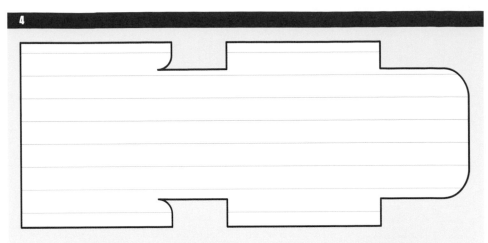

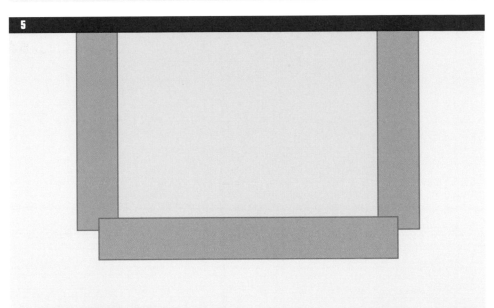

## 5

**2** Assemble the template to test your design and see whether it needs adjustments. Use removable painter's tape on the seams. (After looking at my first design, I modified my template to include rounded corners on the bottom front of the backpack.)

**3** Follow the directions for making a sheet of duct tape on pages 16–17. Create a sheet of duct tape in your main color that's large enough to accommodate the template. If you intend to add pockets to your backpack, add additional length to the sheet.

**4** Trace your template onto the duct tape sheet with a permanent marker. Cut out the design with a rotary cutter or sharp pair of scissors.

**5** Make an interior pocket for a tablet or laptop. Create an 11" × 12" (28 × 30.5 cm) sheet of duct tape in your contrasting color. Apply tape on three sides of the sheet, leaving one of the 11" (28 cm) sides exposed. Center the strips of tape along the edges. Note the square openings left at the lower corners—they will make the tape folding easier in the next step.

**6** Fold the bottom piece of tape up (1). Fold the side pieces of tape in (2). Stick them to the bottom piece of tape at the lower corners to create an adhesive edge along three sides.

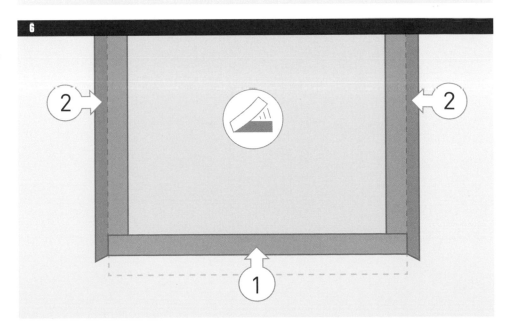

## 6

**7** Center and mark the position for the pocket on the inside of the open backpack. Flip the pocket sheet over and apply it, adhesive-side down, to the backpack as shown. Make sure the open end is toward the backpack's flap. Press the tape in place to secure it. Further secure the pocket by applying a strip of tape around the outside edges.

**8** Make the backpack comfortable with padding on the back. Cut a 12" (30.5 cm) square of foam sheeting. Flip the open backpack over so that the outside surface is facing up and center the foam square under the backpack's flap. Secure the foam sheet with a strip of duct tape along the top and bottom edges.

**9** Further secure the foam sheet with layers of overlapping tape. Trim off the excess tape. You're ready to assemble your backpack.

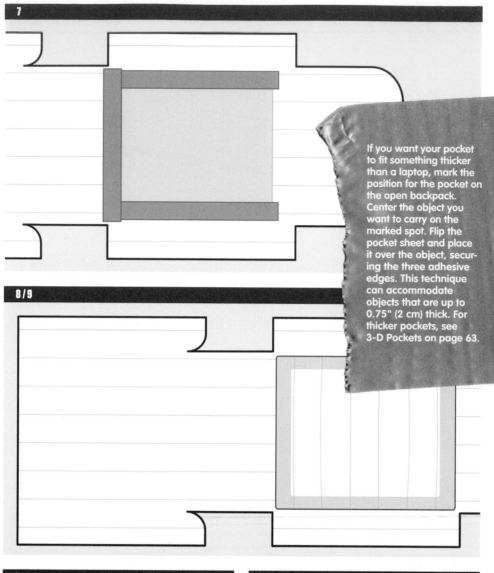

If you want your pocket to fit something thicker than a laptop, mark the position for the pocket on the open backpack. Center the object you want to carry on the marked spot. Flip the pocket sheet and place it over the object, securing the three adhesive edges. This technique can accommodate objects that are up to 0.75" (2 cm) thick. For thicker pockets, see 3-D Pockets on page 63.

## BACKPACK ASSEMBLY

**1** Start with the sides. To attach the curved, lower-front edges, cut an 8" (20.5 cm) strip of tape. Cut the strip in half lengthwise and then crosswise to create four small strips. Fold in one side of the backpack, and begin attaching the curved edge with a strip of tape, as shown.

**2** Bend the backpack to follow the curved edge. Secure it with another small piece of tape. Continue until the entire curved section is secured. Make sure you press the tape firmly into the corner.

Repeat steps 1 and 2 on the other side.

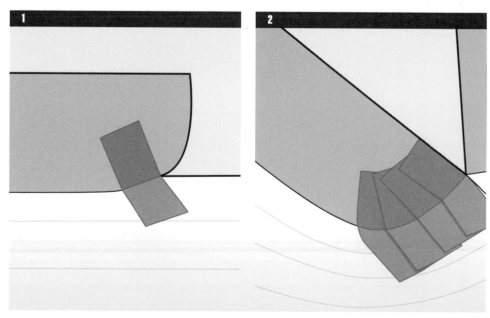

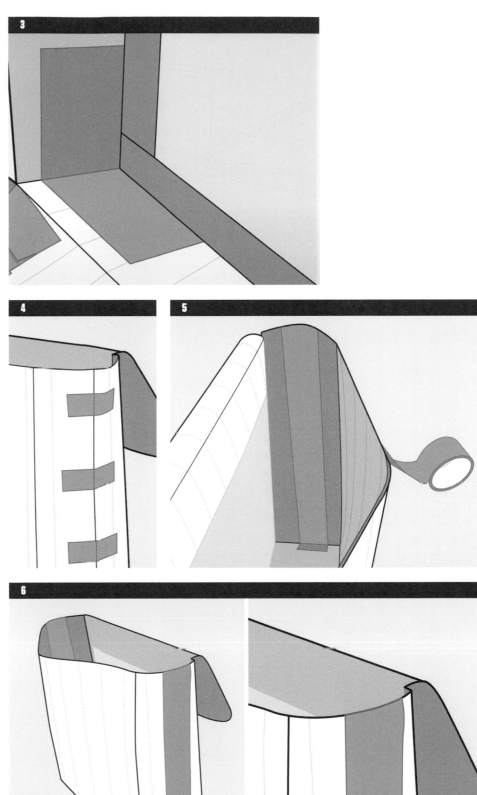

**3** Fold in the other side pieces so they form a right angle with the bottom of the backpack. Attach it in place with a short piece of duct tape.

Again, make sure the tape is pressed into the corner. Repeat on the other side.

**4** Stand the backpack up. Temporarily hold the seam on one side together with five small strips of tape on the outside. For the seam on the opposite side, place five small strips in the same positions, but on the inside of the backpack.

**5** Starting on the inside of the pack, join the first seam with a single long piece of tape. Fold the tape over the top edge and then down along the seam on the outside. Remove the temporary pieces of tape as you close the seam on the outside.

**6** Continue applying tape all the way around the underside of the pack and up the other side. Fold the tape over the top edge and then down the inside of the seam. As before, remove the temporary pieces of tape as you apply the tape on the inside.

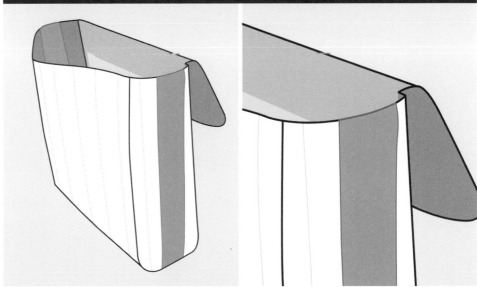

**7** Square up the backpack and fold it flat like a paper bag. Fold the top flap back and trim the top opening of the backpack to even the edge. Open the top flap again.

**8** Reinforce the flap. The flap needs to the reinforced to prevent it from flopping and bending when the pack is closed. Start by cutting a piece of cardboard that is about ½" (1.3 cm) smaller than the flap. Make sure that the corrugations run across the flap, as shown.

**9** Firmly apply overlapping layers of tape parallel to the corrugations in the cardboard. Allow the tape to run off of the flap outline. Trim away the excess tape.

**10** Time to give the backpack its shape. Square up the backpack again, tucking in the sides. Line up the edges of the top opening. Hold the fold down with two pieces of tape.

**11** Place a cutting board or another flat object over the top half of the backpack. Place about 10 lb (4.5 kg) of weight on top. Leave the weights in place for at least two hours. (You can accelerate the process by using heavier objects or by sitting on the cutting board as you read through the rest of this book!)

**12** Remove the weight. The backpack will now fold neatly and naturally at the top.

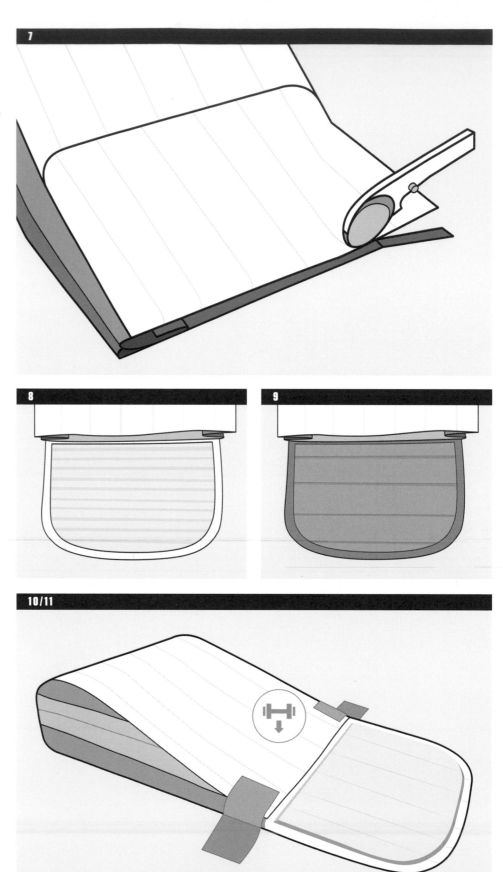

# STRAP TO IT!

**1** Begin creating the shoulder straps by cutting two 15" × 2½" (38 × 6.5 cm) pieces of ½" (1.3 cm)-thick foam.

**2** Center and wrap a single length of your contrasting-color duct tape around each strip of foam. At one end, create a flexible extension by allowing the two ends of the duct tape to overlap and adhere to each other for a length of about 4" (10 cm).

**3** Cover the strap edges with your main color of duct tape. Apply a length of tape along one front edge, about 1" (2.5 cm) in from the edge, wrapping it from front to back. Do the same along the short bottom edge. Trim off the excess tape.

**4** Arrange the straps about 5" (12.5 cm) apart along the top back edge of the backpack. Allow the flexible 4" (10 cm) extensions to fold over the top of the backpack flap. Cover the extensions with overlapping layers of tape, running across the flap. Trim off the excess tape at the edges.

**5** To reinforce the straps, cut twelve 6" (15 cm) strips of your main color of duct tape. Working from the back, lift a strap and apply a strip, connecting the strap to the body of the backpack (1). Repeat with two additional strips in the same place. (Layering the tape will prevent it from ripping over time.) Repeat, layering three strips of tape on the back of the second strap. Do the same with the additional six strips, layering them in two rows between the straps, connecting the flap to the body of the backpack (2).

**6** Apply overlapping layers of tape across the top of the backpack, covering the strips from step 4. Wrap a layer of tape around the top of each strap.

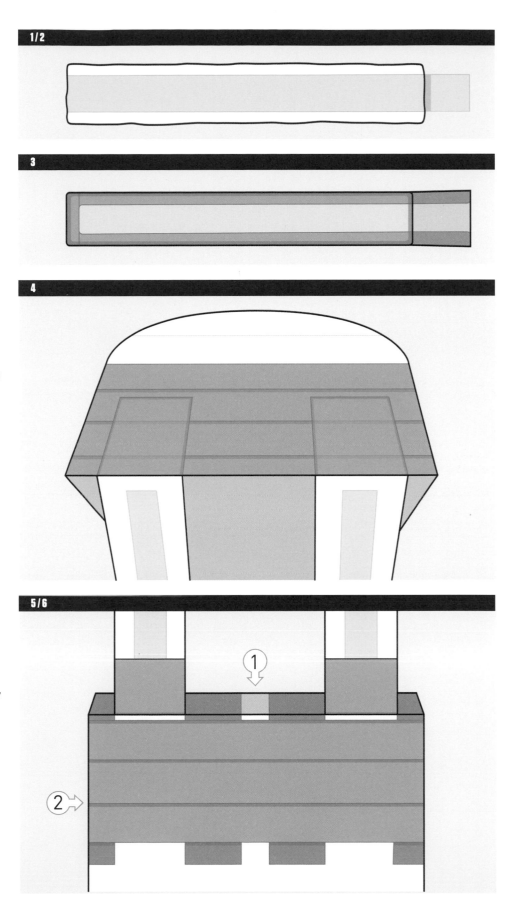

## BUCKLE UP!

**1** Cut a 6" (15 cm) strip of the 1" (2.5 cm) nylon webbing. Thread a strap adjuster over the strip and center it between the ends. Position the webbing, as shown, over the end of the shoulder strap and then hot glue it in place. This will prevent the straps from coming undone over time. Check the strap adjuster's instructions to make sure it's oriented correctly.

**2** Wrap two overlapping layers of duct tape over the webbing and around the strap. Press down on the tape until you can see the texture of the webbing. It will adhere well to duct tape.

**3** Repeat steps 1 and 2 for the second shoulder strap.

**4** Complete the straps by laying two 30" (76 cm) lengths of webbing over the bottom of the backpack at 45-degree angles and then hot gluing them in place. The straps should hang off the back corners of the backpack.

**5** Apply overlapping layers of tape to completely cover the bottom of the backpack. To ensure the webbing is secure, place one hand inside the backpack and press the duct tape onto the webbing until you can see the texture. Trim off the excess tape.

**6** Attach the webbing to the bottom of the backpack with a 6" (15 cm) piece of tape. Forcefully press the tape into the webbing and don't worry about how it looks for now. Repeat on the underside of the webbing.

**7** Tightly wrap another layer of tape around the webbing to secure the previous two pieces. Cover the ends of the wrapped pieces with a fresh layer of tape across the bottom of the backpack.

**8** Insert one length of webbing through a strap adjuster, as shown. Test to make sure it works. Fold back 2" (5 cm) at the end of the webbing and wrap it with tape. This will prevent the webbing from fraying. The straps are done.

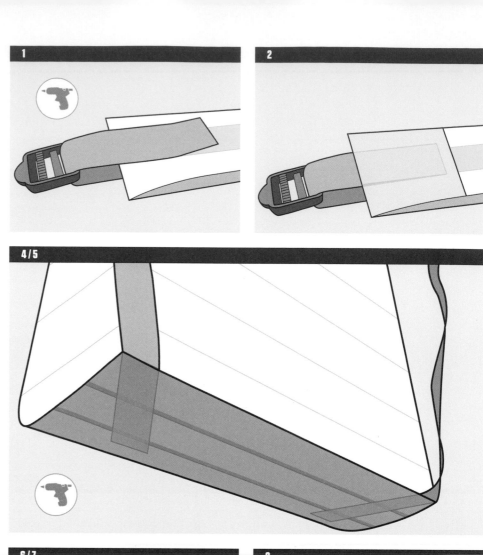

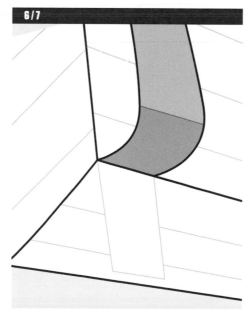

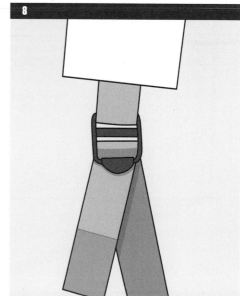

# HOLD ON!

**1**_Create a handle. Cut three 12" (30.5 cm) lengths of your main color of tape. Fold the first piece of tape in half lengthwise. Fold the second two pieces over the first to create a strap that is six layers thick.

**2**_Center the handle, allowing the ends to extend beyond the edges of the backpack. Attach the handle using two layers of tape on each side. The tape should extend from the top of the shoulder strap to the top of the backpack flap.

**3**_Fold the loose ends of the handle strip toward the center (1). Apply two more layers of tape to cover the ends and secure the handle. This technique will prevent the handle from slipping from left to right. Finish it up by smoothing a layer of tape from the top of the shoulder straps to the top of the backpack flap (2).

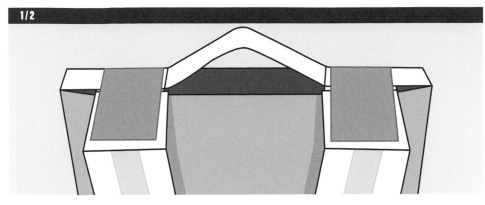

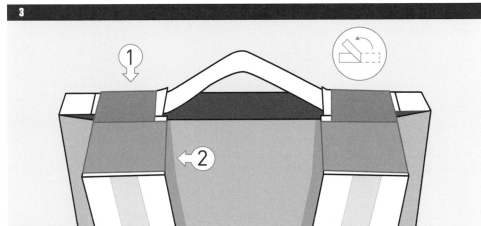

# CREATE THE CLOSURE

**1**_Separate the two pieces of the buckle. Cut a 6" (15 cm) length of webbing and loop it through the open end of the buckle, centering it from end to end. Fold the webbing in half and center the ends over the outside and inside of the flap. Apply overlapping layers of tape to hold it in place. Press down hard to secure the webbing.

**2**_Cut a 12" (30.5 cm) length of webbing. Loop it through the tongue end of the buckle. Center a free end of the webbing on the bottom of the backpack. Apply two long pieces of tape vertically to secure the strap in place, as shown. To further secure the connection, apply layers of tape horizontally over the vertical pieces.

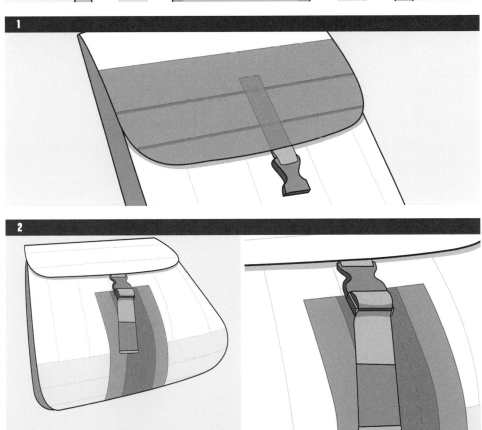

## PICK YOUR POCKETS

Small pockets can be created using the same technique as the large internal pocket (pages 55–56). I've created two exterior pockets from rectangles cut from my original contrasting-color duct tape sheet.

**1** Cut two 3" × 5" (7.5 × 12.5 cm) rectangles from the duct-tape sheet. Following steps 5 through 8 on pages 55–56, apply tape to three edges of the rectangles. Fold the tape in to expose the adhesive side. Adhere the tape at the bottom to create square corners.

**2** Determine the position for the pockets and secure them by pressing with one hand inside the backpack and one hand on the outside.

**3** Secure the outside edges of the pockets with overlapping layers of tape, leaving the top open.

**4** Cut two semicircular pocket flaps from the duct tape sheet. Mine are 3" (7.5 cm) wide and 2½" (6.5 cm) deep. Position a flap above a pocket. Create a duct tape hinge along either side of the top edge of the flap to secure it. Use the adhesive-backed dots to keep the pockets closed. These pockets are perfect for storing keys, cash, cards, and other small items that need to be accessed quickly without opening up the main pack.

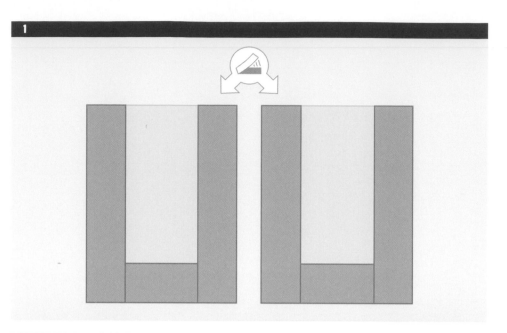

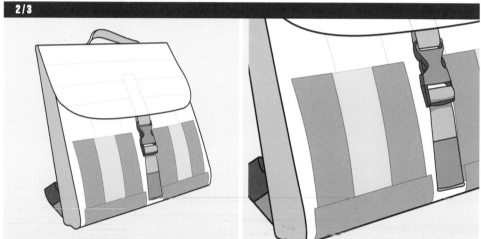

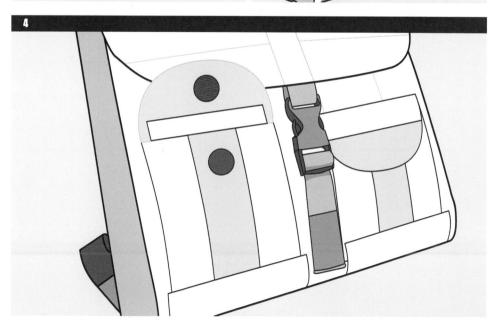

# 3-D POCKETS

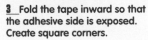

Sometimes you need a little more pocket room inside the backpack for bulky items.

**1**_To create a 3-D pocket, start by cutting a wide T-shape from the duct tape sheet. The size of the bottom corners determines the depth of the pocket.

**2**_Fold and tape the corners together to create a boxlike shape. Apply tape along the inside edge of the sides and bottom of the pocket.

**3**_Fold the tape inward so that the adhesive side is exposed. Create square corners.

**4**_Attach the pocket inside the backpack. Apply tape along the outside perimeter of the pocket, leaving the top open. Use adhesive-backed fastener dots (such as Velcro) to create a closure for the pocket, if desired.

### NOW GET TINKERING!

**These are just a few examples of ways to customize your backpack. Consider adding a water bottle holder or pockets that are designed for specific items, such as your phone. If you're feeling sneaky, create secret compartments that blend in with the surrounding tape, or get really creative and incorporate small speakers, intricate permanent marker designs, or external straps for your camping gear. The ideas to personalize your pack are endless!**

This mega toolbox uses no fancy materials, yet it's capable of storing upwards of 20 lb (9 kg) of tools! Adapt the design to accommodate the tools you rely on all the time, and, if you run out of space, you can always create more pockets and dividers!

# HEAVY-DUTY TOOLBOX

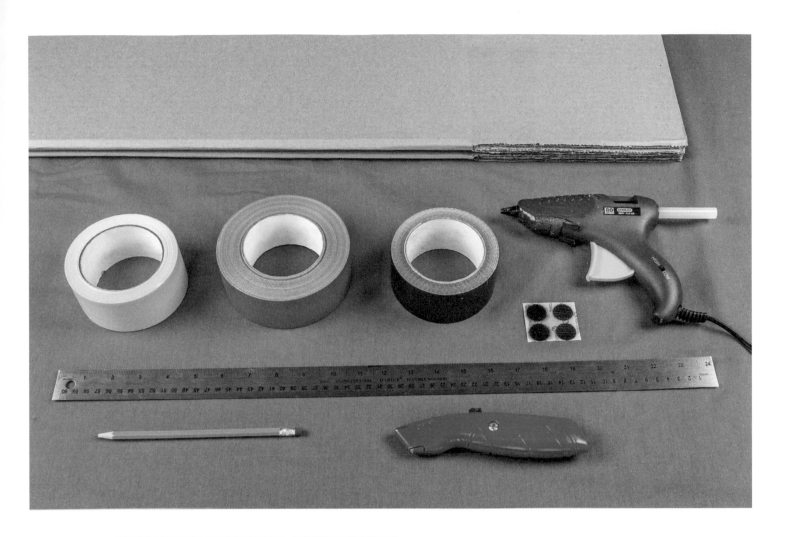

## TOOLS AND MATERIALS

1 HEAVY-DUTY DOUBLE-THICK
CARDBOARD BOX, 18" × 18" × 24"
(45.5 × 45.5 × 61 CM)

UTILITY KNIFE

METAL RULER

PENCIL

20 YARDS (18 M) MAIN COLOR
DUCT TAPE

3 YARDS (2.75 M) SECOND COLOR
DUCT TAPE

HOT GLUE

5 YARDS (4.5 M) THIRD COLOR
DUCT TAPE

2 PAIRS ADHESIVE-BACKED DOTS
(SUCH AS VELCRO)

*This project uses **Duck**® brand's
**Max Strength Duck Tape**® in black
and **Duck**® brand's **Color Duck
Tape**® in yellow.*

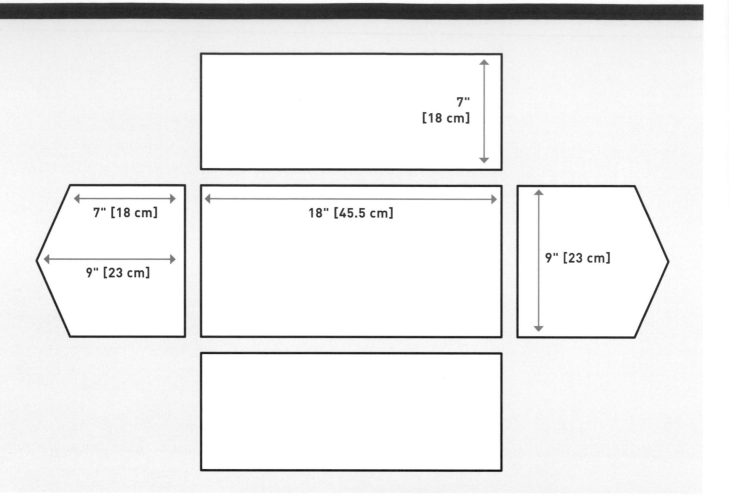

7"
[18 cm]

7" [18 cm]

18" [45.5 cm]

9" [23 cm]

9" [23 cm]

**1** Make the base and sides. Cut the cardboard box along the seam and open it flat on your work surface. Measure and draw the base and sides of the toolbox.

Use a utility knife to cut the pieces. My toolbox has a footprint of 18" × 9" (45.5 × 23 cm), but you can customize the size to your needs. Give the short sides a peaked shape, which allows you to create a tall divider and gives the box an architectural shape.

**2** Cover each piece with your primary duct tape color. Make sure the spaces between the pieces are straight and even. Join the side pieces to the base, taping both sides of every seam.

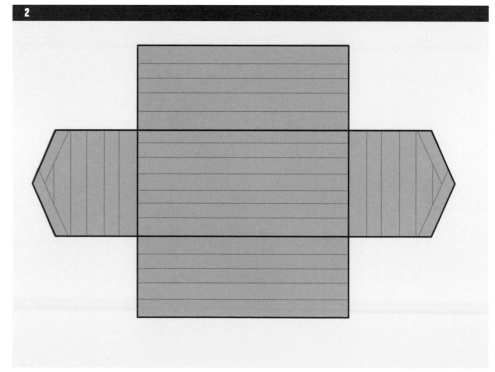

**3** Fold all the pieces together to form the box. Secure the shape by wrapping one long piece of tape around the entire box. Then tape each corner vertically on the inside and the outside.

**4** Make the divider from two identical pieces of cardboard. Measure a rectangle the length of the toolbox base and the depth of the highest point of the sides. Add 4" (10 cm) along the bottom and along the two sides of the rectangle for flaps. Cut the shape. Score the fold lines for the flaps, as shown, and crease them in one direction. Flatten the flaps again and cover one side of the piece with overlapping strips of duct tape. Trim the excess duct tape from the edges. Repeat for a second identical piece.

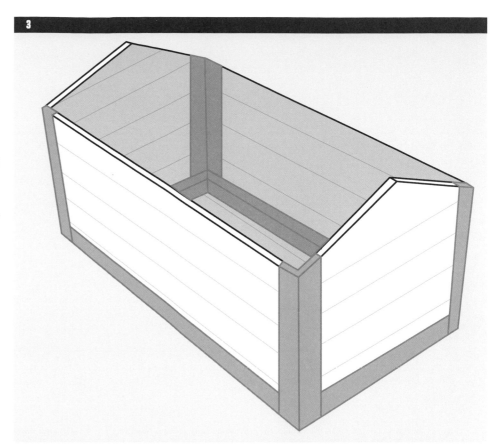

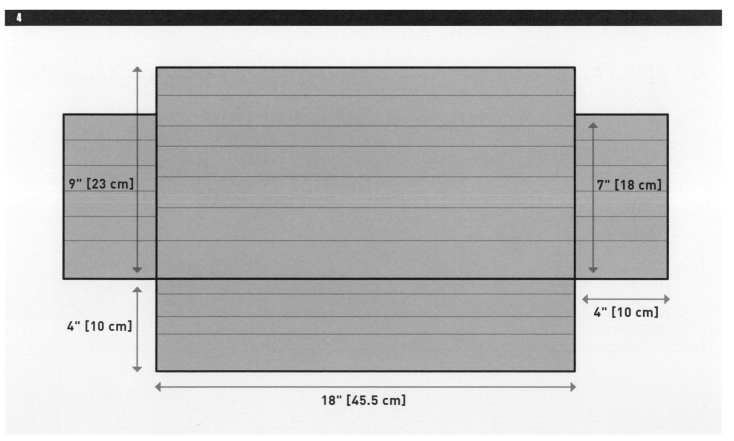

9" [23 cm]

7" [18 cm]

4" [10 cm]

4" [10 cm]

18" [45.5 cm]

**5_** Fold the flaps of both divider pieces outward at a 90-degree angle. Line up the two divider pieces with their untaped sides face to face and hot glue them together. Apply a length of duct tape along the top edge to cover the seam.

**6_** Insert the divider assembly into the toolbox. It should fit snugly. If it's too tight, trim the edges. When the fit is correct, lift each flap and liberally apply hot glue to secure it to the toolbox walls and bottom. Press down on the flaps as the glue dries. This piece needs to be installed securely.

**7_** Make the handle. Cut two 18" (45.5 cm) strips of tape. Fold each in half length-wise. Find the midpoint of the divider. Mark a spot 2" (5 cm) on either side of the midpoint, where the handles will be attached.

Apply hot glue along the 6" (15 cm) end of one handle strip. Attach it to the divider wall, perpendicular to the top edge of the divider. Do the same with the opposite end of the strip, creating a 4" (10 cm)-wide grip. Repeat with the second handle on the other side of the divider. Cover the 6" (15 cm) glued portions of the handles with a 7" (18 cm) strip of tape.

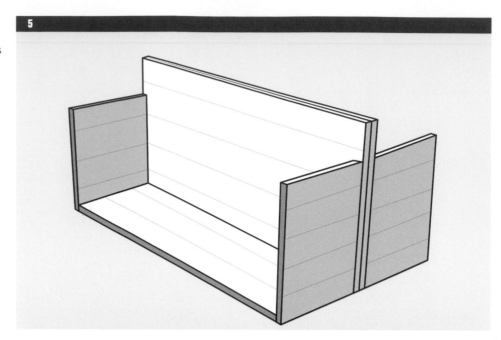

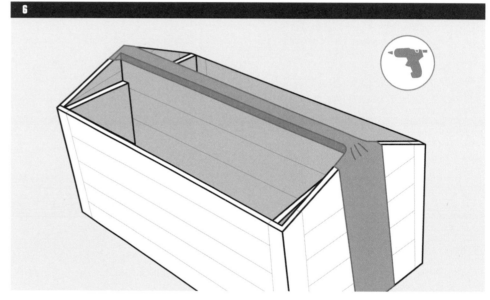

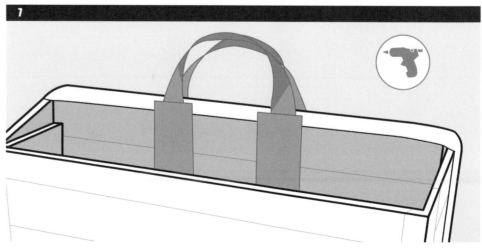

**8** Align the handles so they overlap, as shown. Wrap the two handles together with duct tape to create a single, super-strong handle.

**9** For the pockets, make a double-sided duct tape sheet (see pages 16–17) using your second color of tape. The sheet should be 5" (12.5 cm) wide and long enough to cut out as many 5" (12.5 cm) squares as you want for pockets.

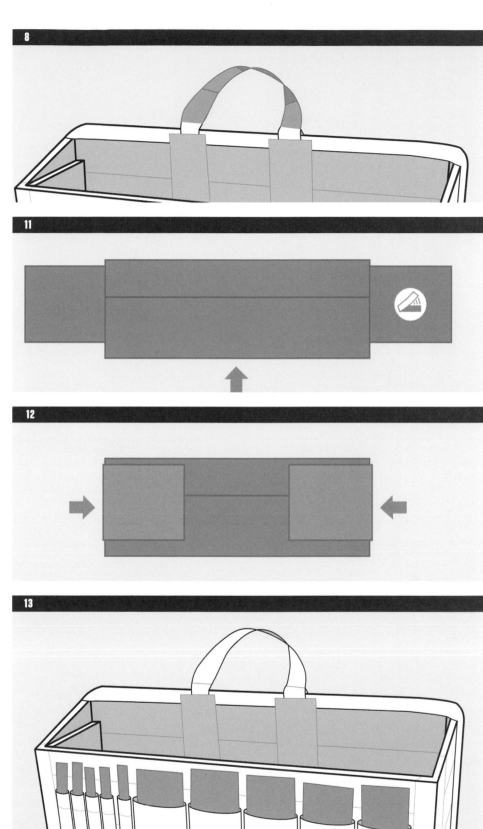

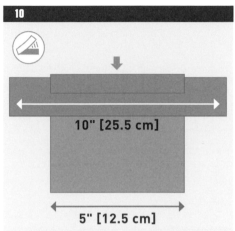

**10"[25.5 cm]**

**5" [12.5 cm]**

**10** Lay one of these squares flat on your work surface. Center a 10" (25.5 cm) strip of duct tape along one side of the square. Move the square so that it over-laps about half the depth of the tape. Fold the taped edge.

**11** Fold the opposite edge of the square onto the tape. Make sure the two edges of the paper align perfectly.

**12** Fold the two ends of the tape over the seam, as shown. You've created one tool pocket.

**13** Create as many pockets as you like for one side of the toolbox. Fashion smaller pockets by using the same tech-nique, but with a tape rectangle that is 3" × 5" (7.5 × 12.5 cm). Apply tape from inside the pocket opening to the top edge of the toolbox, as shown. Make sure the bottoms of the pockets align with the bottom edge of the toolbox.

**14** Create and attach larger interior pockets using the same technique (step 6) used on the toolbox divider. I made my interior pockets from 7" × 7" (18 × 18 cm) squares, cut from a duct tape sheet. Using a third color of tape, wrap a single long piece around the bottom of the pockets. Secure the tops of the pockets with another long piece of tape, as shown.

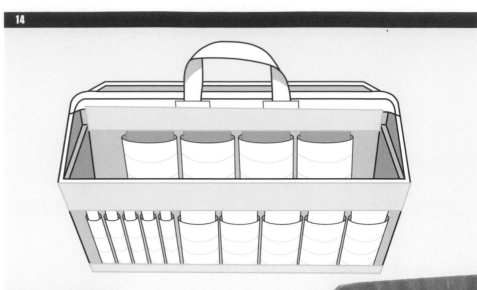

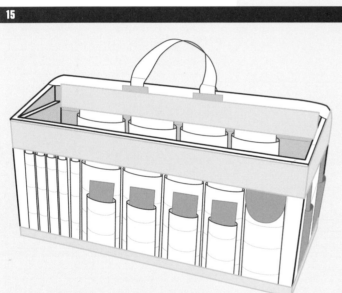

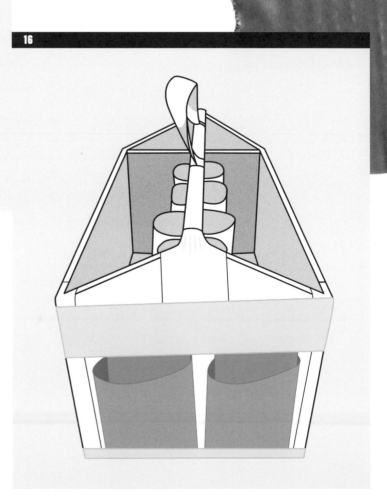

**NOTE**

If desired, attach adhesive-backed dots to close the pockets, as shown in step 4 on page 62.

**15** Use the same technique to build pockets onto pockets! I attached my layered pockets with gray tape on the top and yellow tape on the bottom to match the color scheme. Each layered pocket is attached individually to its parent pocket.

**16** If desired, add more pockets to the other long side of the toolbox. I've made different-size pockets on mine to accommodate specific tools. I've also made a deep 3-D pocket using the technique on page 63 of the backpack project.

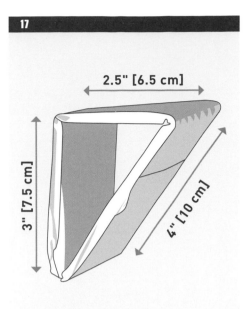

2.5" [6.5 cm]

3" [7.5 cm]

4" [10 cm]

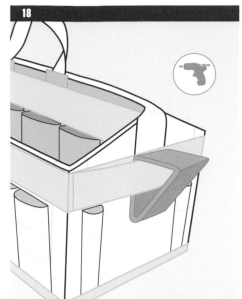

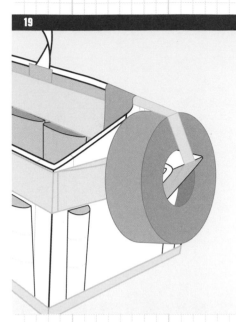

## 18

**17** There's still one unused side of the toolbox, and it's perfect for a special duct tape mount!

Cut a piece of heavy-duty cardboard 9" × 2" (23 × 5 cm). Fold the strip into a triangle as shown. Cover the triangle with tape inside and out.

**18** Center and hot glue the 3" (7.5 cm) side of the triangle to the side of the toolbox. Cut a length of tape long enough to thread through the triangle and wrap around the sides of the toolbox.

**19** Make a strap that's approximately 1½" × 8" (4 × 20.5 cm) by folding an 8" (20.5 cm) piece of tape in half. Tape one end of the strap to the top of the toolbox and then apply a pair of adhesive-backed dots (such as Velcro) onto the other end to secure it to the duct tape mount. Mount your duct tape and strap it on to make sure you're never without it.

**NOW GET TINKERING!**

Everyone's set of tools is unique, so consider your own needs when building your toolbox. All the dimensions of every aspect are customizable. There are also some possible features not shown here, such as a shoulder strap for heavy loads, a water bottle holder, or built-in storage boxes.

Need something other than a backpack for the office? Enter the messenger bag—your stylish solution for transporting academic and workplace necessities. This design is so sleek and stylish, your coworkers will do a double take when they realize it's made almost entirely from duct tape.

# MESSENGER BAG

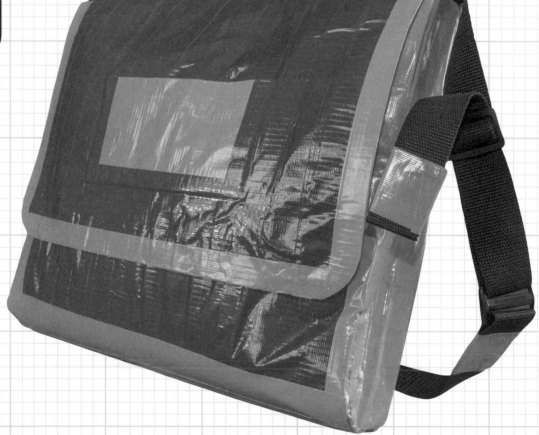

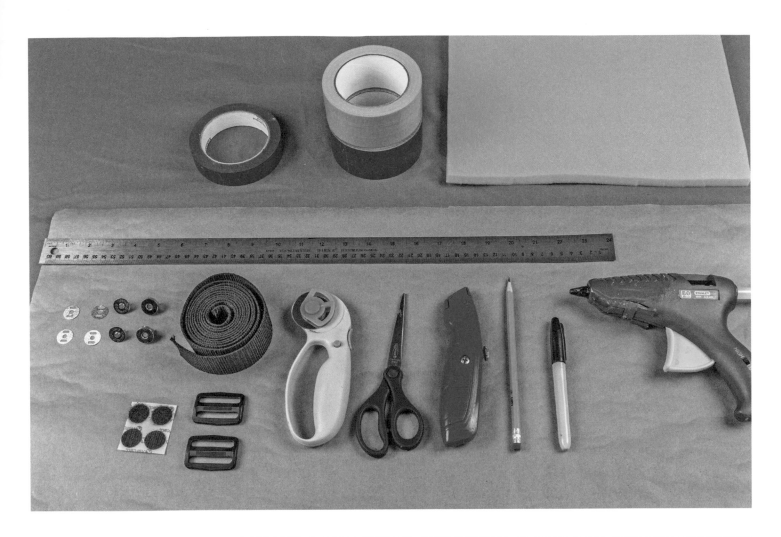

## TOOLS AND MATERIALS

40" (101.5 CM) BROWN PAPER

METAL RULER

PENCIL

SCISSORS

20 YARDS (18.5 M) PRIMARY COLOR DUCT TAPE

PERMANENT MARKER

ROTARY CUTTING TOOL

UTILITY KNIFE

18" (45.5 CM) REMOVABLE TAPE

6 YARDS (5.5 M) SECONDARY COLOR DUCT TAPE FOR TRIM

1" (2.5 CM)-THICK CRAFT UPHOLSTERY FOAM

74" (188 CM) NYLON WEBBING, 1½" (4 CM) WIDE

2 STRAP ADJUSTERS, 1½" (4 CM)

HOT GLUE

AWL

2 MAGNETIC BUTTON CLASPS

PERMANENT MARKER

ADHESIVE-BACKED DOTS (SUCH AS VELCRO)

## MATERIAL SUBSTITUTIONS

You can make the straps entirely from duct tape instead of nylon webbing, but they may not adjust as easily or hold their position as well.

Forgo the strap adjusters altogether and make a static webbing or duct tape strap. Be sure it's the right length for you before attaching it permanently.

This project uses **Duck®** brand's **Color Duck Tape®** in blue and teal.

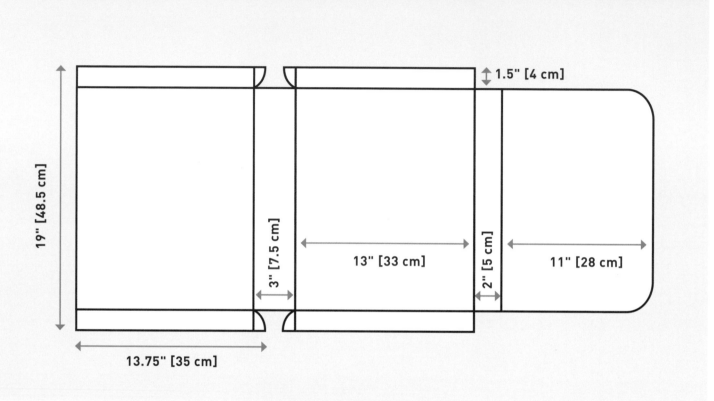

**1.5" [4 cm]**

**19" [48.5 cm]**

**3" [7.5 cm]**

**13" [33 cm]**

**2" [5 cm]**

**11" [28 cm]**

**13.75" [35 cm]**

**1**_Roll out the sheet of brown paper on your work surface. Measure and draw a template for the messenger bag, using the dimensions shown here. Make the six curved corners by tracing the inside of a duct tape roll. Cut the template with scissors.

**2**_Fold the template into the bag's shape, holding the seams together with removable tape. Make sure it's the size and shape you want. If the design needs adjustments, this is the time to work them out on paper.

**3**_Follow the directions on pages 16–17 to create a 40" × 20" (101.5 × 51 cm) duct tape sheet in your main color. If you intend to make pockets, be sure to provide extra space on your duct tape sheet. Lay the sheet flat on your work surface and use the marker to trace the template onto it. Use the rotary cutter to cut the shape.

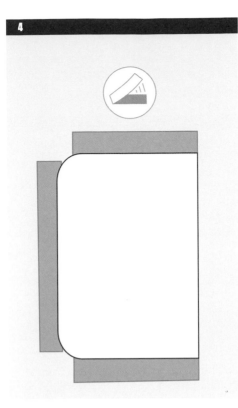

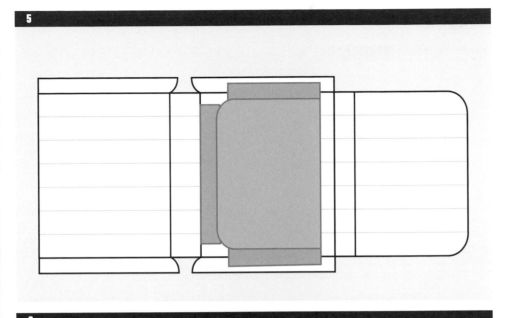

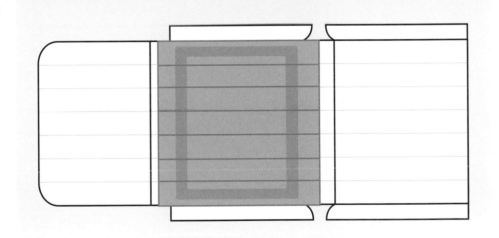

**4**_Make an interior pocket. Lay the cut-out bag on your work surface, interior side up. Follow the directions for the backpack laptop pocket on pages 55–56 to create a pocket in the messenger bag. This pocket is 16" × 11" (40.5 × 28 cm). The rounded corners are traced with the inside of a duct tape roll.

**5**_Continuing with the directions on page 56, center and attach the pocket to the bag. Apply duct tape around three edges, as shown.

**6**_Cushion the bag with upholstery foam. Cushioning the bag where it rests on your hip makes it more comfortable and also helps keep its shape.

Flip the bag exterior side up on your work surface. Cut a 15" × 12" (38 × 30.5 cm) foam rectangle. Center it on the bag. There should be a ½" (1.3 cm) margin around the foam, and it should not overlap the left- or right-side sections. Cover the entire foam pad with overlapping layers of tape with at least a 1" (2.5 cm) margin around all sides.

**7**_Start assembling the bag. Fold in the sides. Use small pieces of removable tape to hold the seams together temporarily.

**8**_Lay the bag flat, with the exterior of the flap facing upward. Center and apply a 17" (43 cm) length of duct tape along one edge of one side piece so that half the width of the tape covers the edge. The tape will span from just above the curved corner, to about 2" (5 cm) above the edge of the bag's opening.

**9**_Lift the bag off the work surface. Fold the tape into the inside of the bag along the seam. Repeat on the other side.

**10**_To tape the curved seam of the bag, begin by attaching a piece of duct tape that wraps around the bottom of the bag with about half of the sticky side of the tape exposed.

**11**_Use the utility knife to carefully cut slits into the tape, spaced about ½" (1.3 cm) apart.

One by one, press each of the tabs in place along the curved surface of the bag.

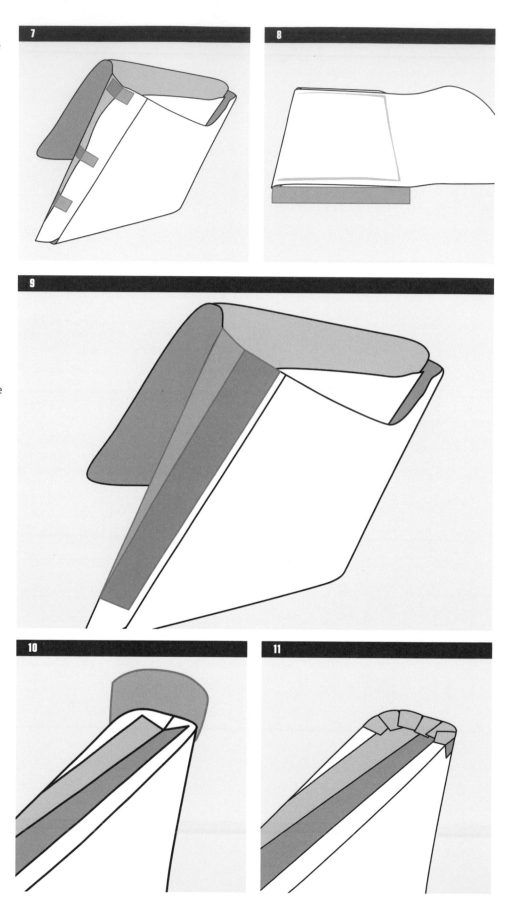

**12** Use the utility knife to cut a curved end on a 15" (38 cm) length of duct tape. Apply the tape to one side of the bag. This helps keep the folded tabs from coming undone. Repeat on the other side.

**13** Apply the trim color duct tape around the edge of the bag's flap. The easiest technique is to fold the tape around the edges and then trim off the corners to conform to the curves. This not only makes the bag look better but also reinforces the edge.

**14** Make the shoulder strap. Cut two lengths of nylon webbing, one 42" (106.5 cm) and one 32" (81.5 cm).

**15** Loop one end of the 42" (106.5 cm) piece of webbing through a strap adjuster. Fold the end of the webbing over and hot glue it to itself. When the glue cools, wrap duct tape tightly around it. This combination of hot glue and duct tape provides a very secure connection.

**16** Weave the 32" (81.5 cm) piece of webbing through the second strap adjuster, as shown, and then through the other side of the first strap adjuster.

**17** Fold the shorter piece of webbing over and then weave it back through the second strap adjuster. Fold and duct tape the end of the shorter piece of webbing to prevent it from fraying.

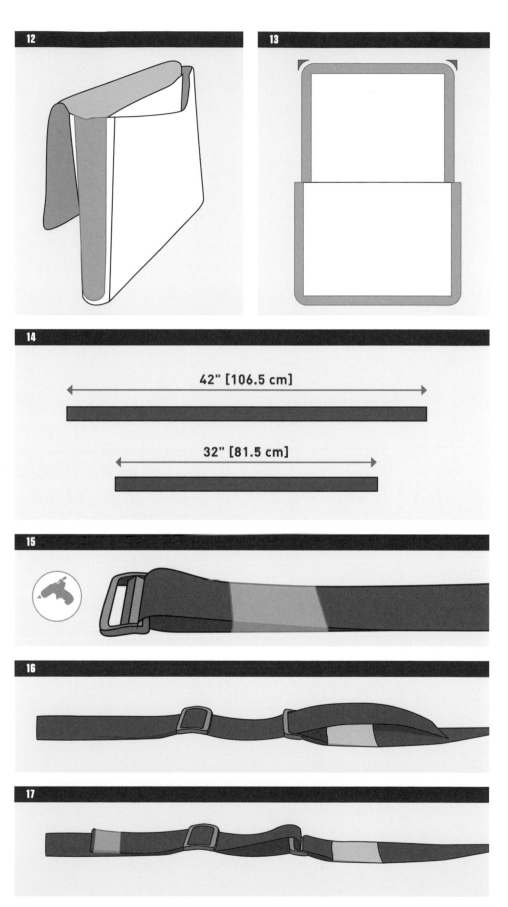

42" [106.5 cm]

32" [81.5 cm]

**18** Hot glue an 8" (20.5 cm) length of the ends of the straps to the sides of the bag. Glue one end at a time, working quickly to ensure the connection is made before the glue dries. Cover the glued section of strap with duct tape. The bag is really starting to take shape!

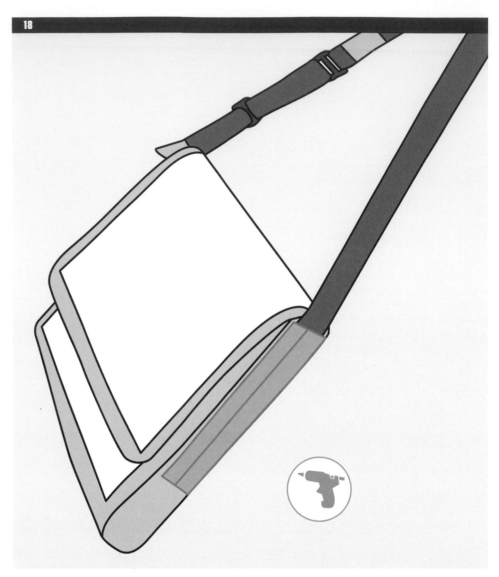

**19** There are a number of ways to add a secure closure for the bag.

I've used magnetic button clasps. I recommend using clasps that attach using tab-and-plate hardware. They are easy to install, require no sewing, and work well with layered duct tape.

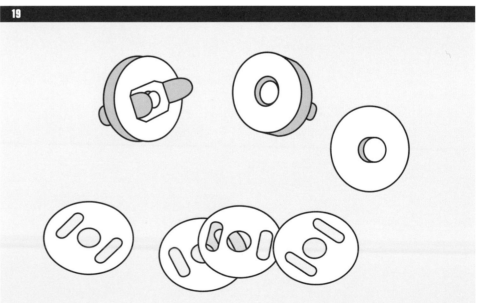

**20** On the inside of the bag flap, mark a dot about 2" (5 cm) from the side of the bag and centered on the edge trim. Use an awl to poke holes on either side of the dot so that the space between the holes is the same width as the clasp tabs. Repeat on the other side of the flap.

**21** Insert the tabs of the male half of the clasp into the holes.

**22** Flip the flap over. Insert the tabs into the metal plate and then bend the tabs completely flat, as shown. This secures the clasp in place. Repeat on the other side of the bag flap. Hide the tabs and plate with a small piece of trim color tape.

**23** Lay the bag down and close the bag opening. Check to make sure the flap closure is resting evenly and naturally. It's important that the flap closure is in its natural resting position or the magnetic clasps won't align. Lift the corner and mark the spot where the center of the clasp touches the side of the bag. Repeat on the other side. If the spot you marked is only two layers of duct tape thick, I recommend applying another layer or two of tape to help it resist tearing over time.

**24** Use the same process to attach the female half of the clasp. The tabs and plate are on the inside of the bag.

**25** Check to make sure the clasps are aligned on one side before following through on the other side.

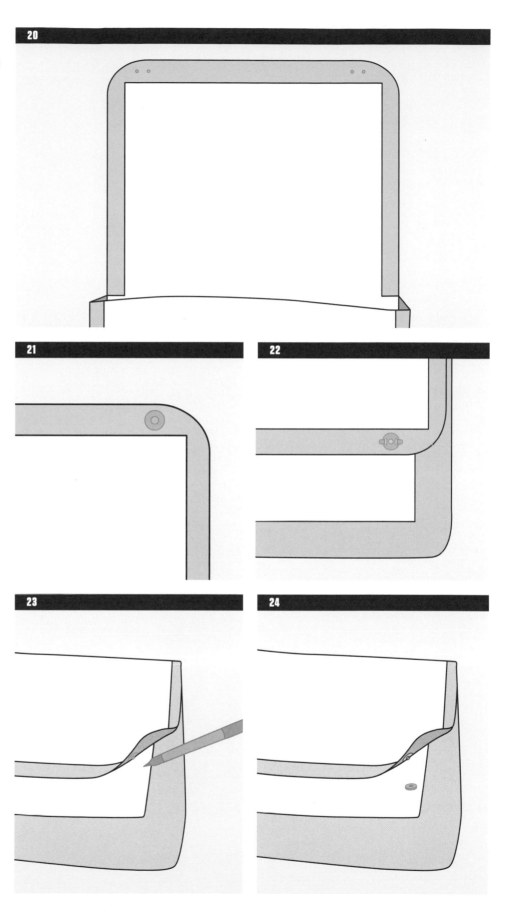

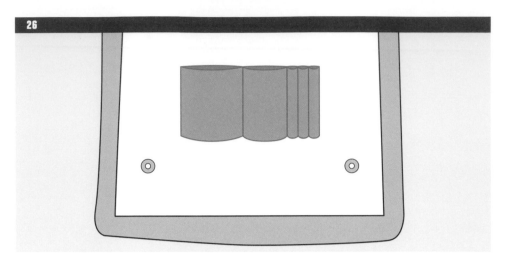

**26** To make exterior pockets for the bag, follow the steps for pockets on page 69. This bag has pockets that are 4½" (11.5 cm)-, 3" (7.5 cm)-, and 1" (2.5 cm)-wide made from a contrasting color.

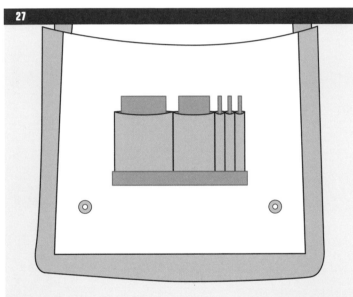

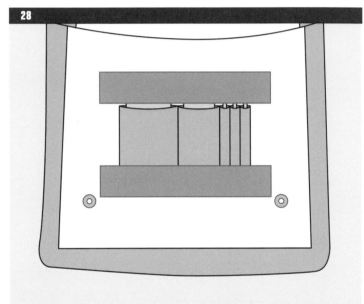

**27** Continue with the directions on page 69 to attach the pockets to the bag. Apply small pieces of tape to attach the inside of each pocket to the bag and one long piece across the bottom of all the pockets.

**28** Cover the tape from step 27 with two long pieces of primary color duct tape.

**29** Add pockets anywhere! This pocket is made using the small pocket technique on page 62. Adhesive-backed fasteners, (such as Velcro) keep the pocket closed.

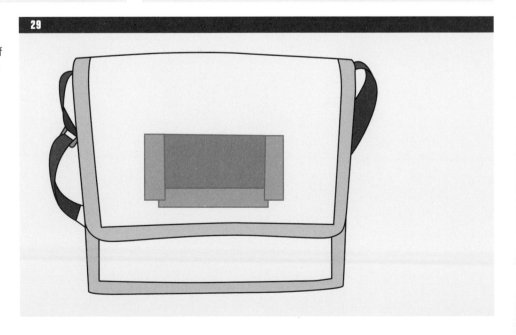

### NOW GET TINKERING!

Like all projects in this book, make it your own. Make a pocket specifically for your phone or tablet or school books and binders. Tape craft upholstery foam to all sides of the bag to make the entire creation cushiony. Get creative with colors and decals. It's yours to make, use, and carry.

# 3 BAC

Step outside and step it up! Here for the making are a hammock, geodesic dome, garden swing, and kayak—all constructed from duct tape and PVC pipe or bamboo! These outdoor projects are epic and among the most challenging this book has to offer. Grab a friend and some cool drinks before digging into one of these massive creations. When you're done, your project will be ready to help you relax and bask in the glow of your ingenuity.

⇨

**INVEST IN
SUN-RESISTANT TAPE**

Regular duct tape breaks
down under sunlight within
a year. If you want your
projects to last, invest in
outdoor-grade tape. Tape
that can resist ultraviolet
light helps your projects
stay standing longer.

# KYARD

Waterproof, durable, and duct tape gorgeous, this hammock is, as always, 100 percent customizable—the combinations of colors and choice of sizes are endless. Your backyard guests will be impressed that the hammock you made yourself can hold up to everyday use.

—

All you need is a sturdy bamboo stake and a couple rolls of duct tape. Construct this hammock with outdoor-grade, UV-resistant duct tape on one side, and colorful standard duct tape on the other. When your hammock is not in use, turn the UV side up to protect it against the sun's rays and keep the colors vibrant.

# HAMMOCK

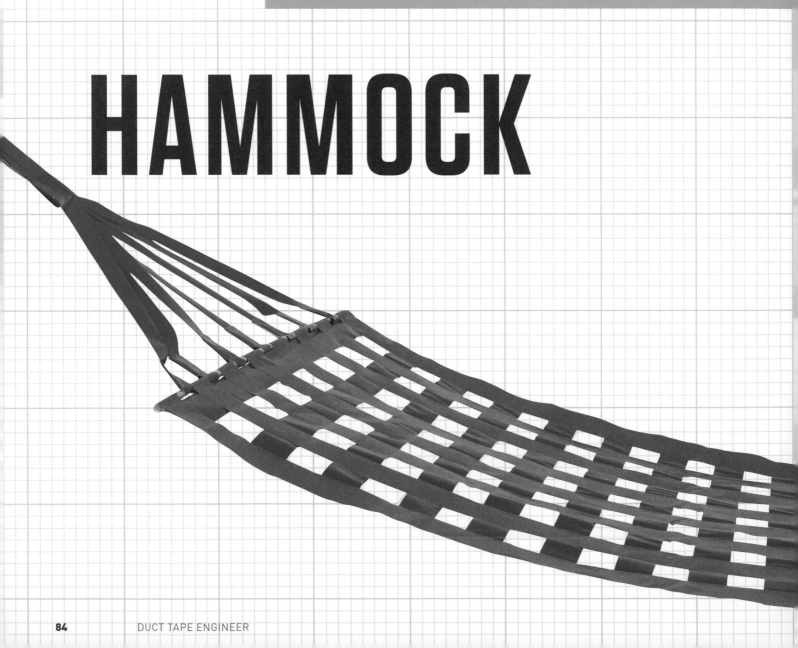

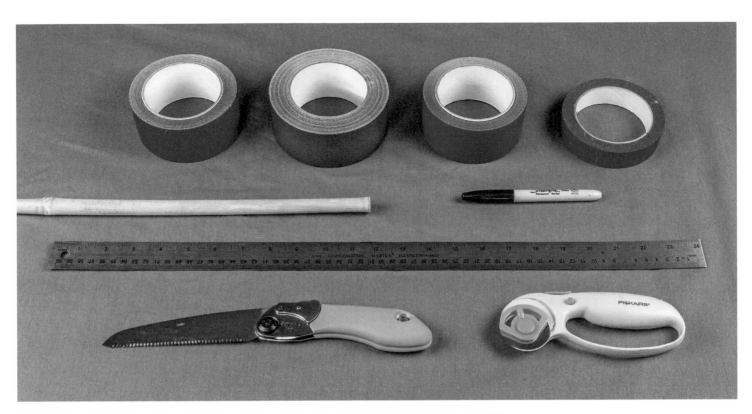

*This project uses **Duck®** brand's **Outdoor Duck Tape®** and **Color Duck Tape®** in blue and red.*

**1** Cut the garden stake into two 3' (91.5 cm) lengths. With the permanent marker, make marks approximately 1.88" (4.7 cm) apart, along the length of each. (This is the width of standard duct tape.) Line up the two stakes 6' (1.8 m) apart on a nonstick work surface and tape them in place with removable tape.

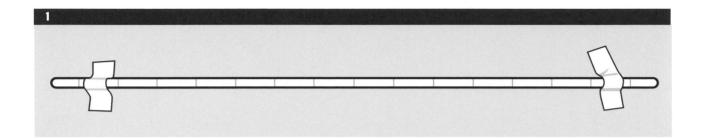

**2** Starting at the outer edge of one of the stakes, lay down one long length of duct tape, attaching it to the stake at either end. Leave a space the width of one piece of duct tape, and then lay down another long length of tape the same length as, and parallel to, the first one. Repeat all the way across to the other end of the stakes.

**3** Apply shorter pieces of tape across the long pieces, forming a checkered pattern. Use a rotary cutter to trim away the excess tape along the long sides. Leave about 2" (5 cm) of tape overhanging the stakes.

**4** Lift the stakes from your work surface and wrap the overhanging tape around each.

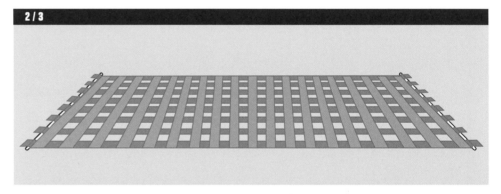

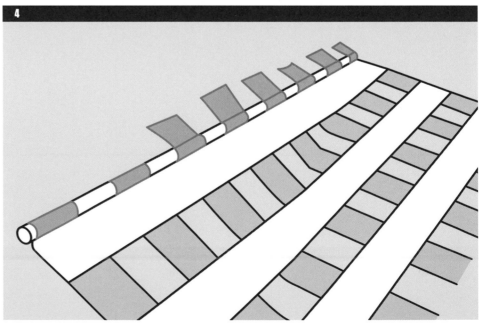

**5** Flip it over. This step is tricky and best done with a partner.

Working with a partner: Each person should hold one of the stakes at both ends. Lift the stakes and gently pry the hammock away from the table. Keep the hammock taut enough that it doesn't fold and stick to itself. Flip the hammock onto its back and lay it flat.

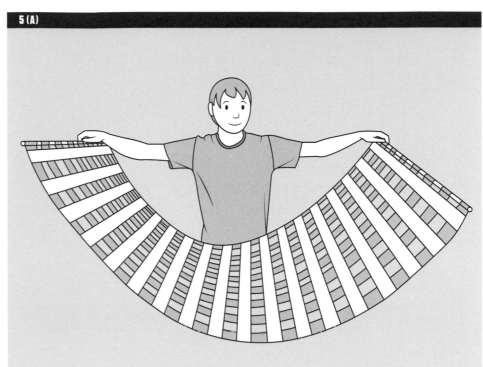

5 (A)

5 (B)

Working solo: Hold onto both stakes and carefully lift the hammock to pry it from the table (A).

Raise one stake high above the other. Make sure the stakes remain parallel to prevent the tape from sticking to itself (B).

Bring the higher stick across the lower one. Drop the lower stick and switch hands. Continue bringing the higher stick across the lower one. The sticky side of the tape should now be facing upward. Use your free hand to pull the lower stick in the opposite direction, and then lower the hammock back onto your work surface (C).

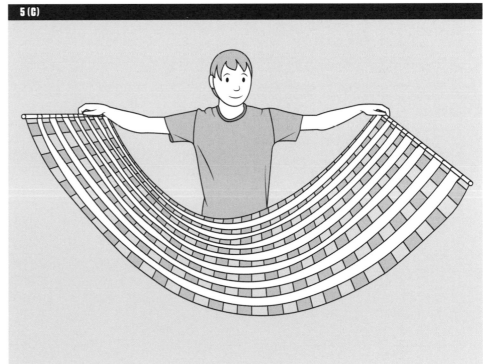

5 (C)

**6**_Tape the opposite side. You'll now apply fresh tape to the sticky side of the hammock. Be as accurate as possible: You will not be able to pull two pieces of duct tape apart without damaging the hammock.

Start with the shorter pieces. Unroll a length of duct tape wide enough to span the width of the hammock. Hold the tape at both ends. Lean over the hammock to get an accurate top-down view of the strip you're aiming for. Hover the tape over the strip to make sure it's aligned and then carefully lower it.

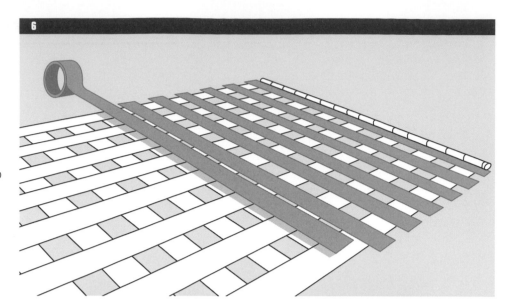

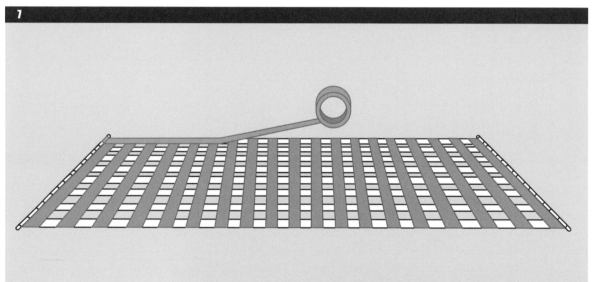

**7**_Apply the long pieces. Unroll about 12" (30.5 cm) of tape at one end. Look directly over the section you are about to tape. Press the tape into place as you go, working toward the opposite stake. Continue unrolling and applying 12" (30.5 cm) lengths of tape until you reach the end. This technique is more manageable than trying to apply the entire 6' (1.8 m) section at once.

**8**_The hammock mesh is complete!

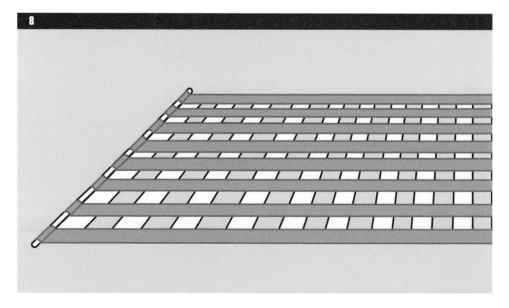

**9** Create the support straps. Lay a 3' (91.5 cm) length of duct tape on your work surface, sticky-side up. (Taping the ends in place prevents it from moving.) Lay another strip of duct tape on top of the first, sticky-side down. Smooth the two to seal the bond. Use a rotary cutter to cut the strips in half lengthwise. Repeat six more times to create a total of fourteen 3' (91.5 cm) straps.

**10** Loop each strap around a stake. Fold the end back toward the strip, over-lapping the strip by at least 2" (5 cm). Use outdoor-grade duct tape to attach the end to the strip.

**11** Cut an 8" (20.5 cm) length of outdoor-grade duct tape in half lengthwise. Pull all the hammock straps toward the center and bundle them with a piece of the outdoor-grade tape. Repeat at the other end.

**12** Carefully straighten and stack the straps.

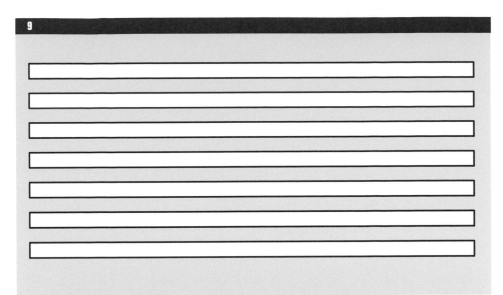

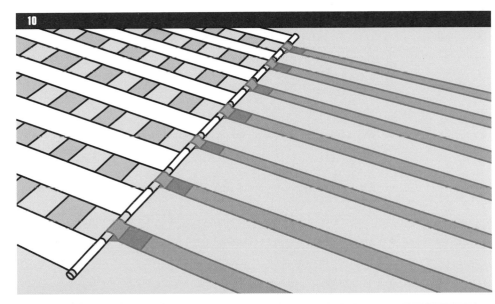

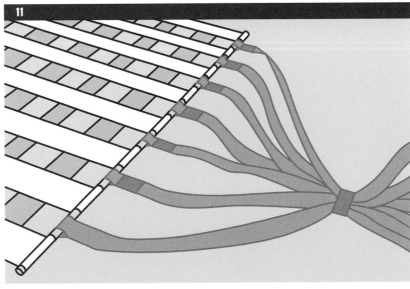

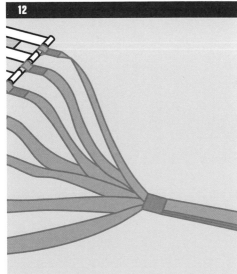

**13** Fold the stack into a loop. Use outdoor-grade tape to bind the loop. Trim any long tails, but leave about 12" (30.5 cm) of the straps extending beyond the binding.

**14** Fold the 2" (5 cm) strap ends back against the loop. Wrap outdoor-grade duct tape around the fold to hold it in place. This S curve of the tape prevents the strap bundle from slipping loose over time.

Your straps may appear a little crooked. This is normal. As the hammock gets used, the straps will stretch and straighten out.

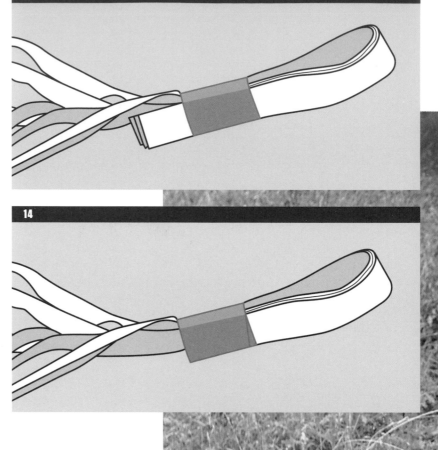

As with all projects in this book, this is just one way to do it. You could use this same idea to create a giant hammock or a treetop lounge!

A geodesic dome in my backyard, you ask? What could be more practical? You can easily make a dome any size you want for, say, a walk-in greenhouse, a playhouse for the kids, or a cozy outdoor shelter.

—

Geodesic domes are the perfect balance of simplicity and sophistication. Although complex in appearance, they consist only of an arrangement of triangular panels. The sole challenge is ensuring that the triangles are the right size, but, fortunately, we've made the math super easy. Get ready to transform a minimum of materials into an epic-scale duct tape project!

# GEODESIC DOME

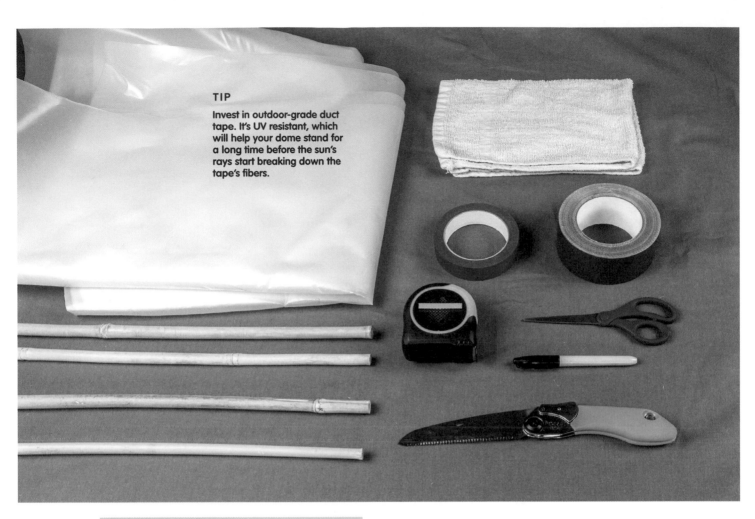

TIP

Invest in outdoor-grade duct tape. It's UV resistant, which will help your dome stand for a long time before the sun's rays start breaking down the tape's fibers.

## TOOLS AND MATERIALS

**37 BAMBOO GARDEN STAKES, 6' (1.8 M) LONG AND ½" (1.3 CM) WIDE**

**MEASURING TAPE**

**PERMANENT MARKER OR PENCIL**

**FINE-TOOTH SAW OR HEAVY-DUTY GARDEN LOPPER WITH A CURVED BLADE**

**REMOVABLE BLUE PAINTER'S TAPE**

**AT LEAST 180 YARDS (164.5 M) OUTDOOR-GRADE DUCT TAPE**

**DRY CLOTH**

**1 ROLL PLASTIC SHEETING, 10' (3.5 M) WIDE, 6 MIL (25.40 µm) THICK**

**SCISSORS**

*This project uses **Duck®** brand's **Outdoor Duck Tape®** in silver.*

NOTE

Garden bamboo works well because it's inexpensive, durable, and has a smooth surface, which is a good match for duct tape. The challenge with bamboo is that it splinters easily. Use a fine-tooth saw to cut it. Heavy-duty garden loppers will splinter the wood a bit, but the ends will eventually be wrapped in tape, so a small amount of splintering won't matter.

## GETTING STARTED

**1** Decide on a dome pattern. You can find them on the internet. The example here is a plan known as V2, which requires only two different lengths of bamboo and is easy to build. In this top-down diagram, the red lengths are shorter than the blue lengths.

**2** Calculate the length you'll need to cut your bamboo poles. The math is pretty simple. First decide on the diameter of your dome. This dome is 10' (3.5 m) across.

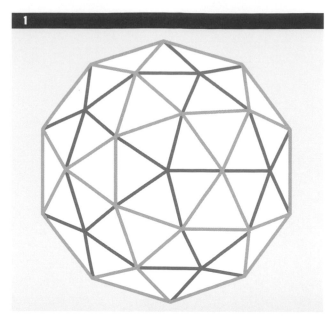

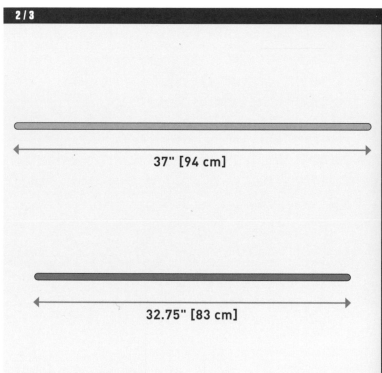

37" [94 cm]

32.75" [83 cm]

**3** Measure and cut the pieces. You'll need thirty-five long pieces and thirty short pieces. Mark one length with blue tape to help keep track of your plan. In this example, I've marked the long pieces with blue tape to match the color in the diagram.

### GEODESIC MATH

Here's a little help to calculate the correct length of your dome pieces.

For the long pieces, multiply the diameter of your dome in inches (or centimeters) by 0.309.

For the short pieces, multiply the diameter of your dome in inches (or centimeters) by 0.273. Round to the nearest quarter inch (or centimeter).

For example, let's look at the long pieces: The dome's diameter is 10' (3 m), which equals 120" (305 cm).

Long pieces = 120" × 0.309 = 37.08" (305 cm × 0.309 = 94.25 cm)

Short pieces = 120" × 0.273 = 32.76" (305 cm × 0.273 = 83.25 cm)

# GEODESIC DOME TAPING TECHNIQUES

## END-TO-END CONNECTIONS

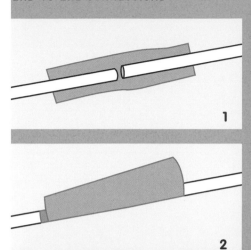

To connect bamboo poles end to end, begin with a long piece of duct tape that overlaps the ends of both poles (1). Include a ¼" (0.6 cm) gap between them. You'll need this gap to allow the bamboo to flex at the corners. Wrap the tape around both pieces. Wrap a second piece of tape over the first to secure the joint further (2).

*Tip: Always wipe the bamboo with a cloth before applying tape. Small amounts of dust, grease, or other contaminants prevent the tape from adhering as strongly as possible.*

## OVERLAP CONNECTIONS

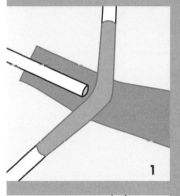

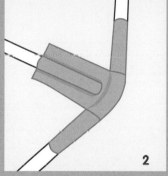

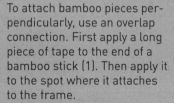

To attach bamboo pieces perpendicularly, use an overlap connection. First apply a long piece of tape to the end of a bamboo stick (1). Then apply it to the spot where it attaches to the frame.

Fold the tape around the bamboo and stick it to itself (2). Wrap a second piece of tape around the first piece (3).

This last step is optional, but it will make the connections cleaner and stronger.

## CORNER CONNECTIONS

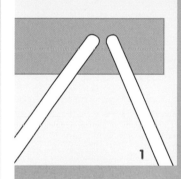

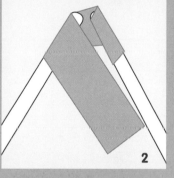

To connect triangular corners, start by creating the corner on one end of a long piece of tape (1). Wrap the short end of the tape around one side. Wrap the long end of the tape around the other side and simultaneously pull it taut toward the middle of the triangle (2). Tightly wrap the tape under and over the corner. Wrap the remaining length of tape tightly over the top tip of the corner (3). This technique may take a little practice, but it is well worth it to have super-strong connections.

This project is much easier and goes a lot faster if you can build it with a partner.

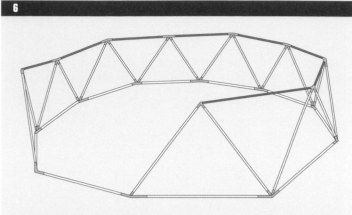

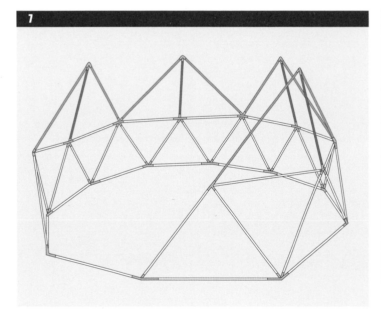

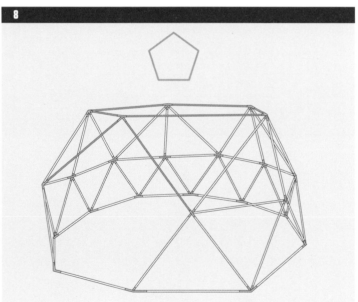

**4** Form the circumference of the dome's foundation by connecting ten long pieces of bamboo end to end.

**5** Use the taping connection techniques shown on the preceding page to create nine triangles. Leave a space where the tenth triangle will go—this will be the dome's doorway.

For each triangle, use two overlap connections to attach each piece to the foundation. Use one corner connection to bind the top of the triangle together.

**6** Form a second ring, as in step 5, this time using eight short pieces of bamboo joined end to end. Stand the triangles up as you go. Use overlap connections to secure the second ring to the top of the first row of triangles. It's fine if your dome doesn't stand up on its own at this point. It may continue to be wobbly until the final pieces are added.

**7** Create a new round of triangles. Use two long pieces of bamboo (shown in blue) for the sides of each and a short piece (shown in red) for the center brace. Use overlap connections to attach pieces to the upper ring, and corner connections to connect the tips of the new triangles. Keep a close eye on your pattern and make sure these pieces are being connected in the correct arrangement as shown.

**8** Attach another ring, connecting five long pieces of bamboo. Once it is secured, the dome should be able to stand on its own.

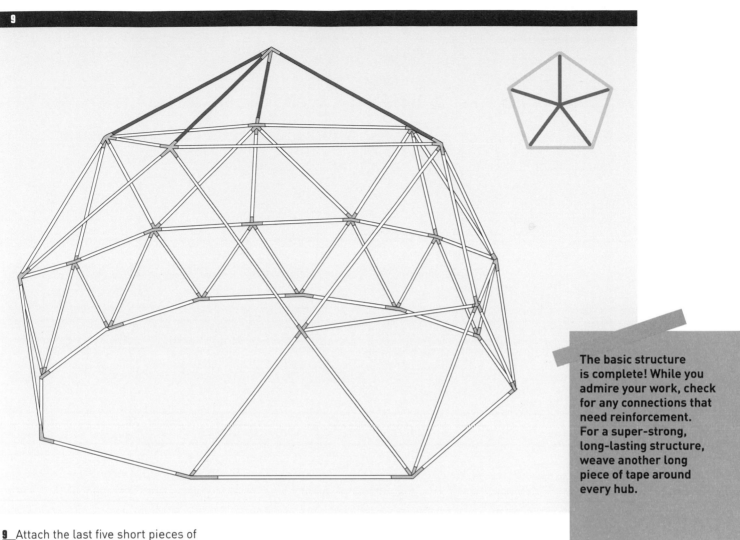

The basic structure is complete! While you admire your work, check for any connections that need reinforcement. For a super-strong, long-lasting structure, weave another long piece of tape around every hub.

**9** Attach the last five short pieces of bamboo to form the apex of the dome.

**10** Support the door frame. Measure the distance from the bottom edge of the door frame to the upper door frame pole. Cut two pieces of bamboo to this length and then duct tape them in place with overlap connections, as shown. These pieces will be a little different for each dome. In this example, they are about 38½" (98 cm) long.

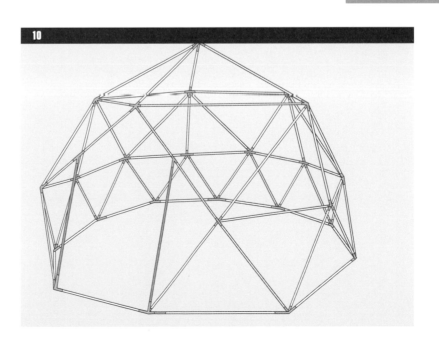

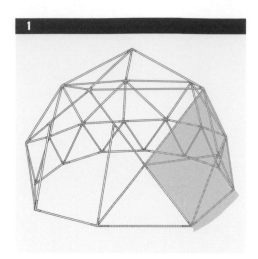

## 10

## COVERING THE DOME

**1** Drape a large piece of plastic sheeting over one of the pentagons that make up the perimeter of the dome. Temporarily hold the plastic in place with small pieces of duct tape. Keep the plastic as taut as possible. Use a permanent marker to trace the outline of the pentagon onto the plastic.

**2** Trim off four sides of the pentagon. Apply another small piece of tape to keep the plastic in place. Leave the bottom uncut for now. Keep the plastic as taut as possible.

**3** To remove any slack in the plastic, pull the plastic taut in the lower section of the pentagon. With the marker, draw a line from the center of the pentagon to the bottom edge. Cut the plastic along the line. Pull the excess plastic taut over the cut and trim off the excess. For now, continue to use small pieces of tape to hold the edges of the plastic in place along the edges of the pentagon. Repeat with all of the pentagons as shown in the next step.

**4** Use a cloth to wipe the plastic and then use long pieces of tape to secure each edge of the plastic to the bamboo sides of the pentagons. As always, keep the plastic taut as you work. Tape the edges of every pentagon.

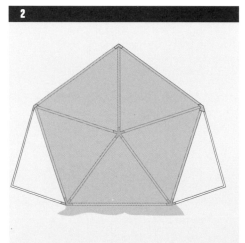

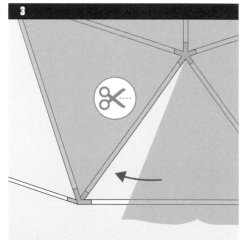

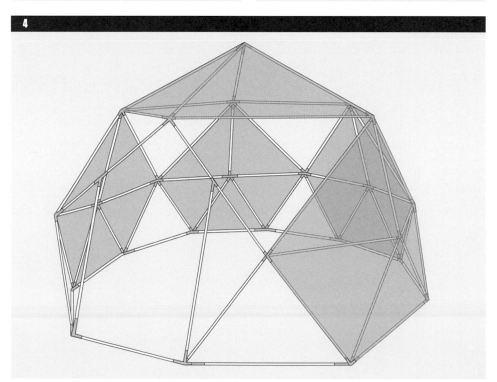

**5** To tape the pentagon seam, first trim away the plastic so it does not overlap the bamboo.

**6** Apply a piece of tape to both the inside and the outside. For a strong connection, place one of your hands inside the dome and press your hands on both sides of the tape. If there are spots where the plastic is covered by less than ½" (1.3 cm) of tape, apply another long piece of tape.

**7** Cover each remaining triangle by draping a scrap of plastic over it, holding the plastic in place with small pieces of tape. Outline the triangle with a marker while keeping the plastic taut. Cut off the excess.

**8** Apply duct tape to the inside and outside of the triangle seams. If there are spots where the plastic is covered by less than ½" (1.3 cm) of tape, apply another long piece of tape.

**9** Using the same technique as the other triangles, cover the remaining gaps at the doorway. The plastic covering is complete!

**10** For a finishing touch to the look, I added outlines in tape where there were none.

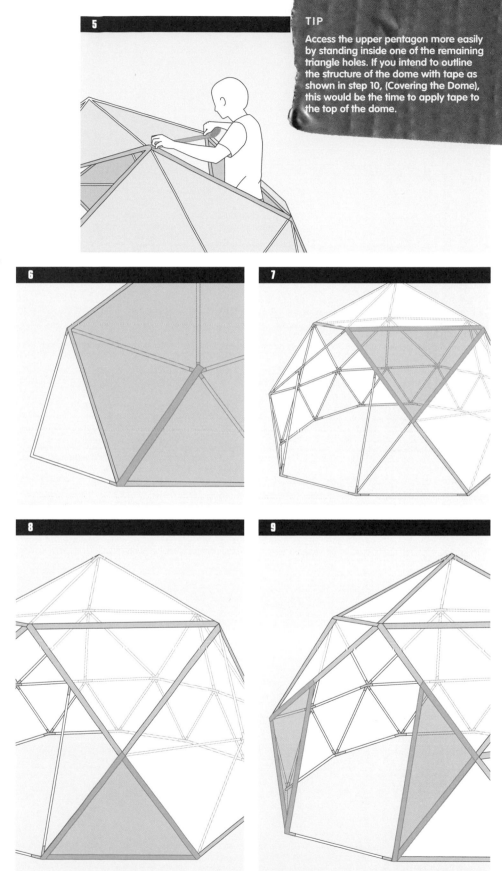

TIP

Access the upper pentagon more easily by standing inside one of the remaining triangle holes. If you intend to outline the structure of the dome with tape as shown in step 10, (Covering the Dome), this would be the time to apply tape to the top of the dome.

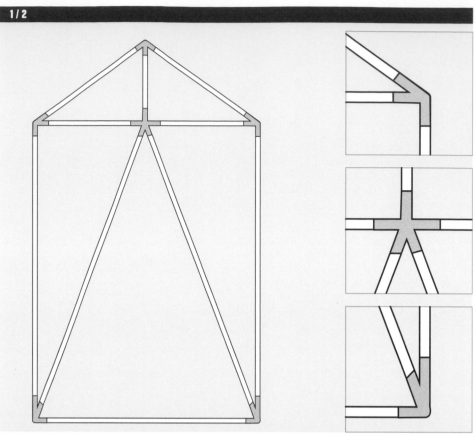

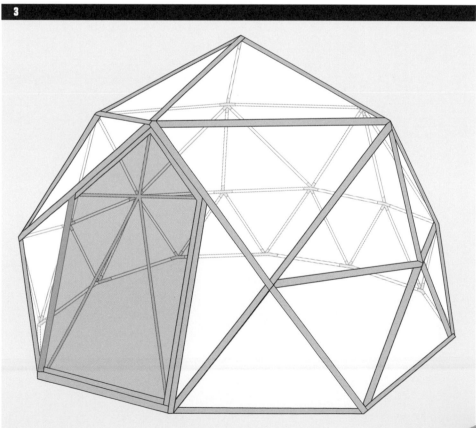

## BUILD A DOOR [OPTIONAL]

**1** Measure the five sides of your doorway. Cut five pieces of bamboo that are approximately 1" (2.5 cm) longer than each dimension you just measured. This will ensure that the door covers the doorway.

**2** Join the five bamboo pieces with end-to-end connections to form an irregular pentagon. Lay the door flat. Measure and cut four more bamboo poles and then tape them to the interior of the pentagon, as shown. This makes the doorway rigid, and this pattern fits with the aesthetics of the dome's structure.

**3** Cover the door in plastic and then apply duct tape along the inside and outside of one edge to create a hinge.

***You're finished!***
Customize your dome by adding windows, or simply enjoy it by filling it with lounge chairs, a table for drinks, and greenhouse plants.

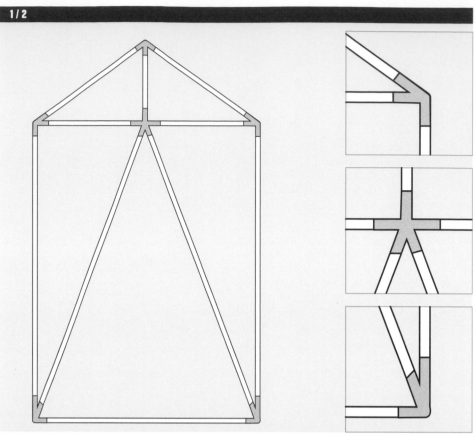

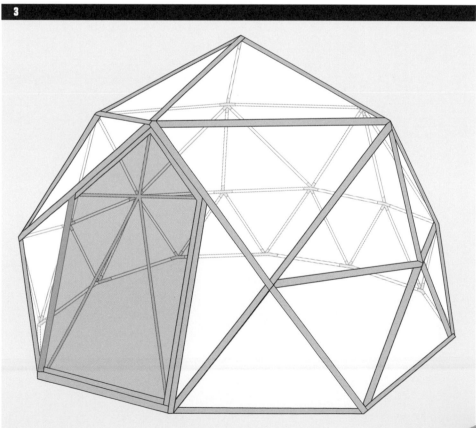

This structure is designed to last about two years in mild weather. If you live in a climate with frequent rain, consider adding additional layers of overlapping tape to the inside and outside seams. Please note that this structure hasn't been tested in snow or prolonged, high-heat weather.

From a short distance away, you'd never know that this project is made from only duct tape and bamboo. It looks lightweight but can hold up to 250 lb (113 kg)! As such, you need to use the best quality tape. This project uses ShurTech® brand's T-Rex Tape®.

—

Most of the joints in this load-bearing structure are wrapped at least twice. If you use regular duct tape to make the swing, apply tape to a larger area around each joint, and wrap each joint many more times to ensure a bond strong enough to hold the weight of one or two people. This is a truly epic project that requires time and a lot of tape, but the payoff is worth it.

# GARDEN SWING

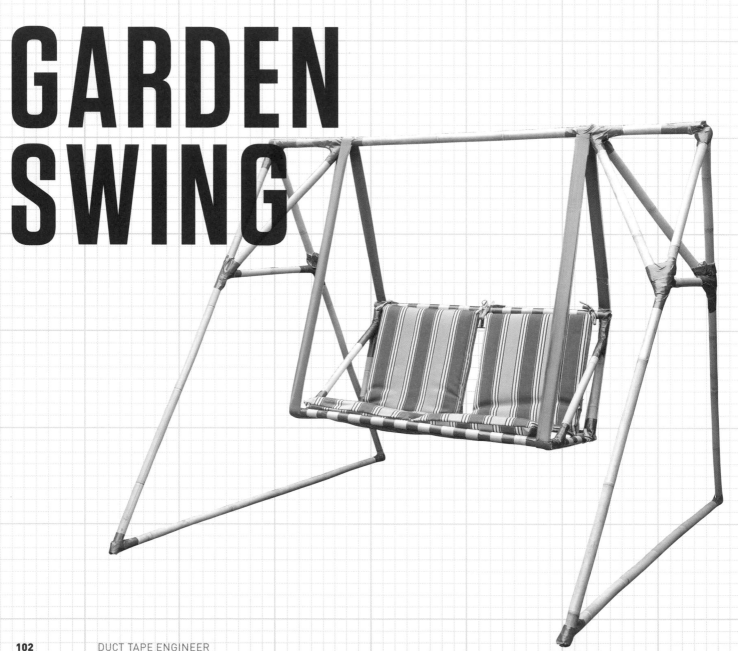

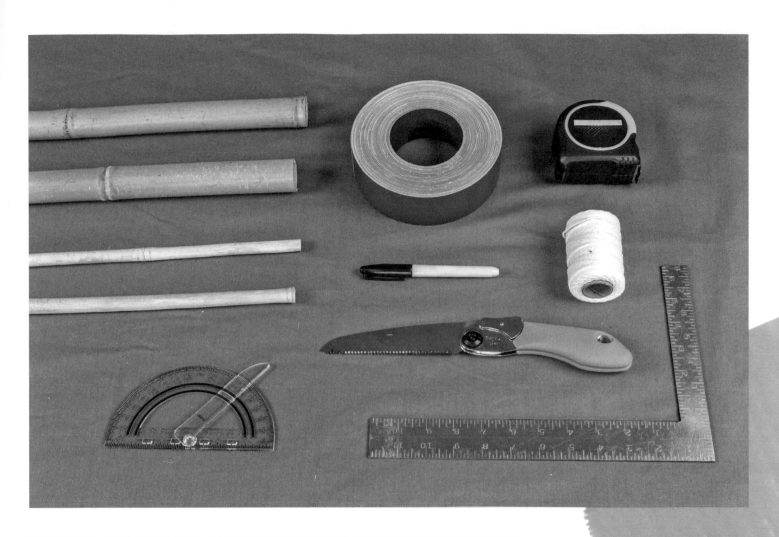

Use heavy-duty outdoor tape for this project.

## TOOLS AND MATERIALS

**12 BAMBOO POLES, 6' (1.8 M) LONG, 1½" (4 CM) THICK**

**PROTRACTOR**

**PERMANENT MARKER**

**GARDEN SAW**

**3 ROLLS SHURTECH® BRAND'S T-REX TAPE®**

**MEASURING TAPE**

**STEEL SQUARE**

**3 BAMBOO GARDEN STAKES, 6' (1.8 M) LONG AND AT LEAST ½" (1.3 CM) THICK**

**STRING**

## MATERIAL SUBSTITUTIONS

You can use any saw, besides a garden saw, that can cut through thick bamboo; a saw with deep saw-tooth height is recommended.

*This project uses **ShurTech®** brand's **T-Rex Tape®**.*

## BUILD THE SWING'S FRAME

**1** Start by constructing the swing's A-frame supports. Use a protractor to mark a 30-degree angle at the ends of six of the 1½" (4 cm)-thick bamboo poles. Use the garden saw to cut along the angled lines. Start your cuts slowly to avoid splintering.

**2** Arrange the cut ends of the poles flush to form two equilateral triangles.

**3** Join three corners of each A-frame by wrapping the joint tightly with an 8" (20.5 cm) piece of tape. Repeat at least one more time on the other side to maximize the coverage.

**4** Make the center braces for the A-frames. For each brace, cut a 1½" (4 cm)-thick bamboo garden pole to 24" (61 cm). Mark the ends at 60-degree angles, and be sure the marks mirror each other. Cut along the marks.

The braces should fit snuggly between the two sides of each A-frame. The height of the brace should be the same for each frame.

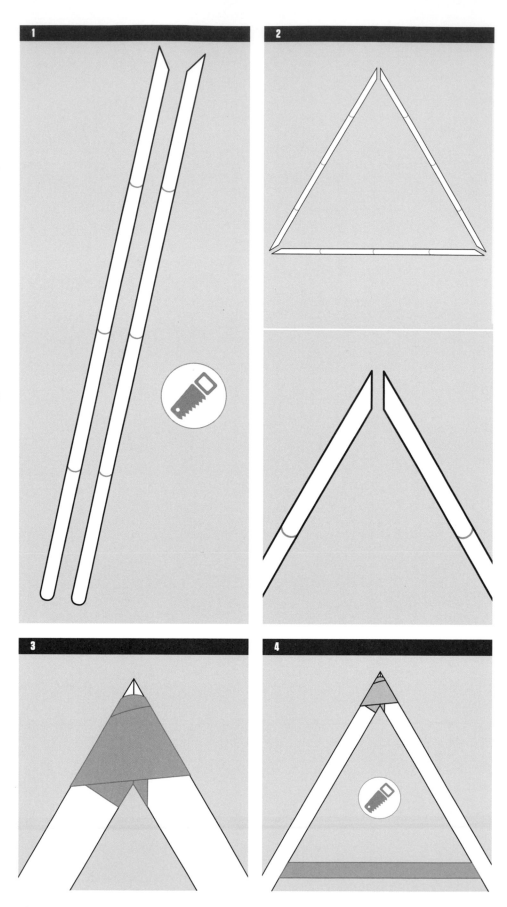

**5**_ Cut four 6" (15 cm) pieces of tape. Secure the center braces in place by applying a piece of tape to either side.

**6**_ Wrap the tape over the sides of the A-frame.

**7**_ Tightly wrap another piece of tape around the A-frame poles and the undersides of the center braces. Repeat two more times to ensure the tape won't rip under stress.

**8**_ Add the top pole to connect the two A-frames. Cut a 100-degree notch from the apex (top peak) of each A-frame. The notch will support the pole.

**9**_ Wrap more tape around the joint at the top of each A-frame to ensure the weight of the top pole doesn't split the joints. Start by placing a 6" (15 cm) piece of tape on the side.

**10**_ Wrap the tape tightly around the sides, and then do the same on the reverse side. Repeat steps 9 and 10 at least two more times.

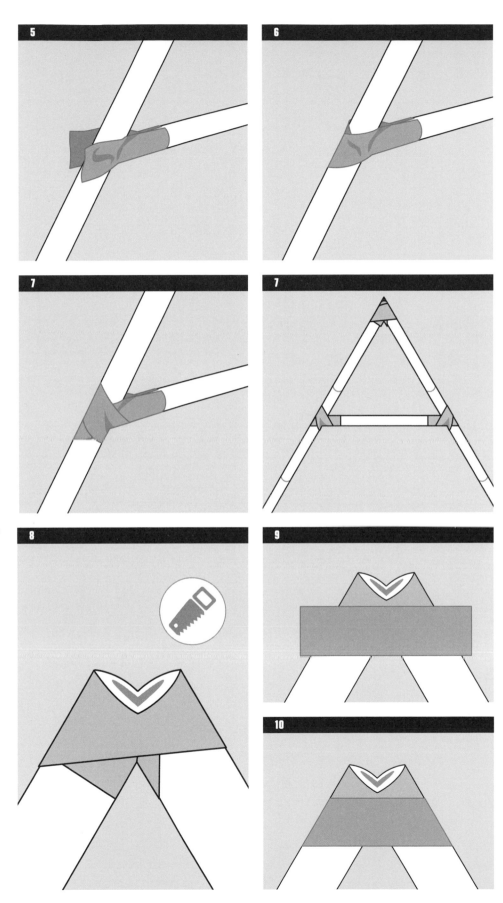

**11** Add the top pole. Prop up the A-frames about 6' (1.8 m) apart. Rest the pole on top, fitting it into the notches.

**12** On each end of the A-frame, wrap a 12" (30.5 cm) piece of tape from the top of the top pole, around two sides of the frame, and then under the top pole.

Secure the tape by wrapping a fresh 8" (20.5 cm) strip of tape around the top pole at each end.

**13** Further secure the tape by pressing another 8" (20.5 cm) piece of tape over each apex and down the sides.

Repeat steps 12 and 13 at least two more times to prevent the pole from slipping out of place.

**14** Four diagonal braces will keep the frame stable. Begin building the braces by cutting four 28" (71 cm) pieces of the 1½" (4 cm)-thick bamboo pole. Mark and cut a 25-degree angle at one end of each and a 60-degree angle at the other end.

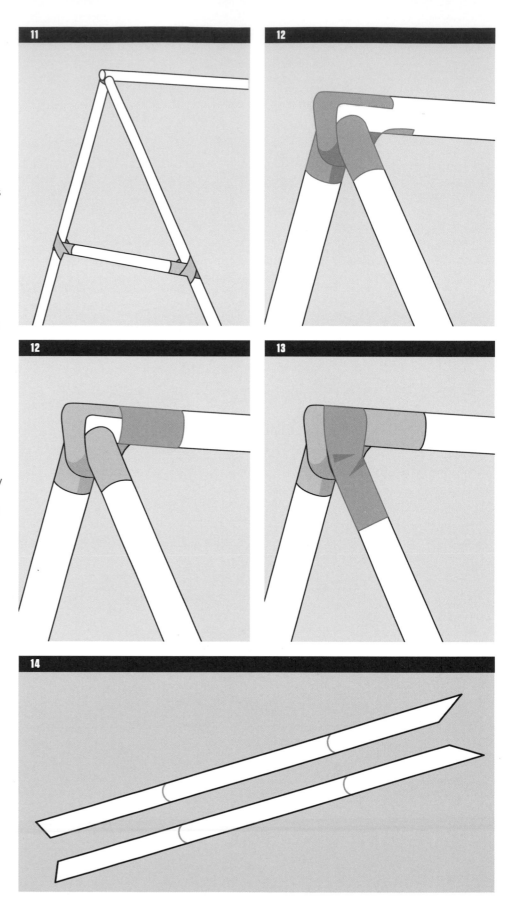

**15** The 25-degree cut connects to the A-frame, and the 60-degree cut connects to the top pole. Use small pieces of tape to hold one diagonal brace in place. It should reach from about the height of the side brace on the A-frame to about 14" (35.5 cm) in along the top pole.

**16** **The connections at each end of the diagonal braces need to be extremely secure.** The braces transfer most of the load from the swing into the A-frame poles. Begin by wrapping tape around the diagonal brace and *over* the side brace of the A-frame. Pull tightly on the tape as you wrap it to ensure it lies neatly over the poles.

**17** Repeat the wrapping technique from step 16, but this time wrap the tape **under** the side brace of the A-frame.

**18** Wrap another length of tape over the previous piece and around the A-frame pole. This prevents the previous layer of tape from slipping down the pole over time.

**19** Apply one more layer of tape to fill in any gaps and prevent water and debris from collecting inside the joint.

Repeat steps 16 through 19 to double the strength of this connection. Repeat the entire process with the second diagonal brace at this end of the frame, as shown.

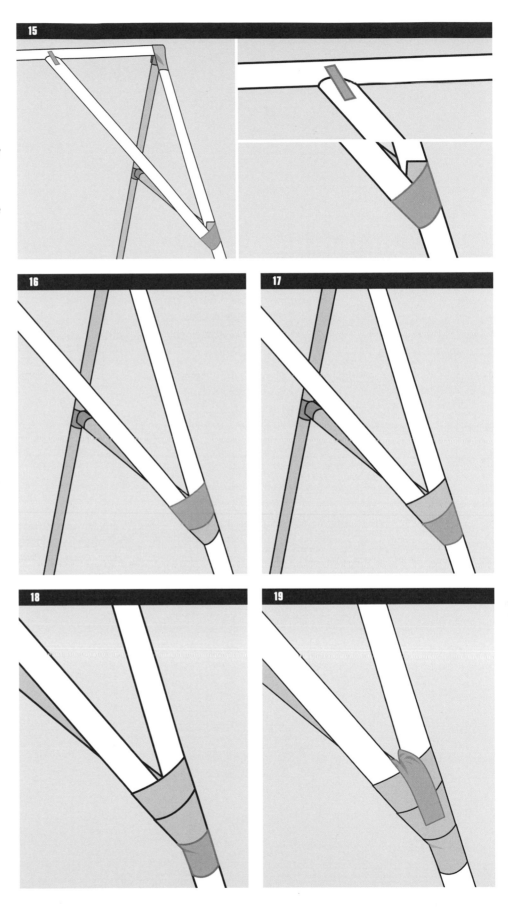

**20** Still working at the same end of the frame, attach the diagonal braces to the top pole with two 8" (20.5 cm) pieces of duct tape to hold them in place. These pieces are just to ensure that the braces are in the right position.

**21** Cut a 12" (30.5 cm) piece of tape. Attach it to the top pole. Wrap it around both diagonal braces and to the other side of the top pole.

**22** Attach another piece of tape in the same way. Cut this piece to 10" (25.5 cm) and apply it at a steeper angle.

**23** Apply an 8" (20.5 cm) piece of tape that attaches along the side of one brace and wraps over the top pole. Repeat with the other brace. Repeat steps 21 through 23 one more time.

**24** Finish by wrapping 8" (20.5 cm) lengths of tape around both braces and on both sides of the top pole where it connects with the braces. This prevents the tape from slipping due to stress, or peeling due to moisture and sun exposure over time.

**25** Repeat steps 14 through 24 with the two braces at the other end of the swing frame. The frame is done!

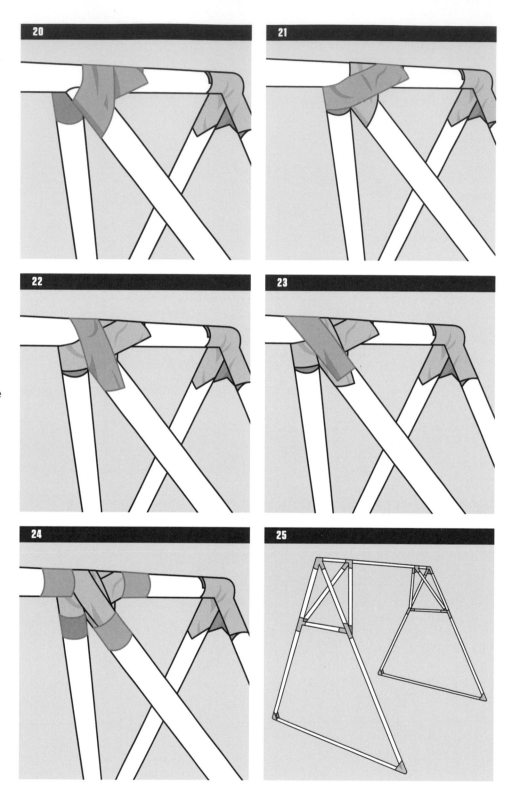

# MAKE THE SWING

**1** The swing is made with a sturdy seat and back. Begin constructing the seat by cutting two 43" (109 cm) pieces and two 28" (71 cm) pieces of 1½" (4 cm)-thick bamboo. Arrange them in a rectangle, as shown. Note the ends of the short pieces are butted against the long pieces.

**2** Wrap 8" (20.5 cm) lengths of tape over each corner as shown. Wrap a second piece of tape over the first piece to secure it.

**3** For the swing's back, cut one 43" (109 cm) piece of 1½" (4 cm)-thick bamboo and two 28" (71 cm) pieces. Follow steps 1 and 2 to construct the back of the swing like the seat but with one open side.

**4** Position the back and seat of the swing, as shown. Apply duct tape to the front and back to hold the joints securely. Repeat once more to double the thickness of the tape connections.

**5** Wrap the joints with tape.

**6** Place the swing on the floor and prop the back to keep it upright. Decide on the angle of the back by pulling the seat frame toward or away from the chair. This example is leaning back at a comfortable 80-degree angle.

**7** Add braces to permanently position the angle of the back. Begin by cutting two 1½" (4 cm)-thick bamboo poles to 24" (61 cm). For an 80-degree-angled back, mark and saw the ends at 40 degrees. Hold the braces in place with two small pieces of tape.

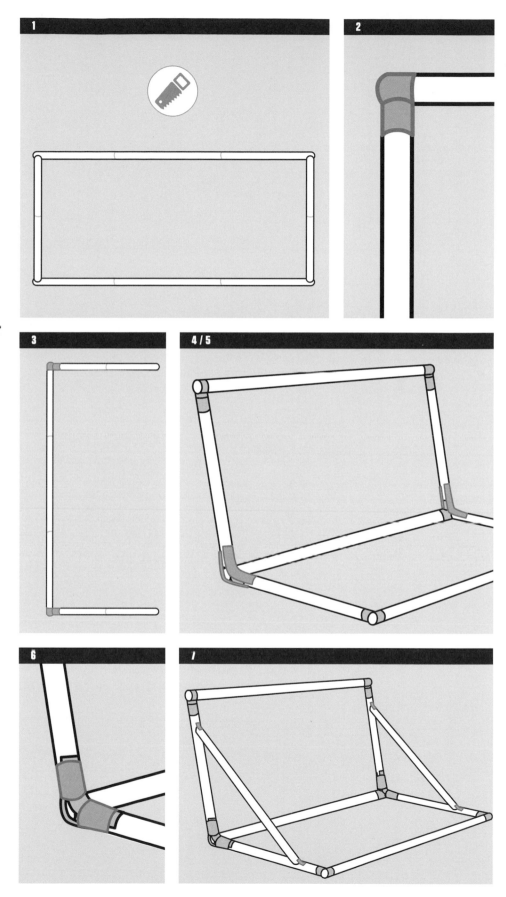

**8** Attach the bottom of the brace to the seat by applying a 6" (15 cm) piece of duct tape, as shown. This prevents the brace from slipping forward over time.

**9** Wrap an 8" (20.5 cm) piece of tape around the brace and the seat.

**10** Cut a 12" (30.5 cm) length of duct tape. Center it on the underside of the seat below the brace joint. Wrap each end of the tape over the top of the brace.

**11** Finish the connection by wrapping tape around the joint from step 8 once more, as shown. This further prevents the brace from slipping over time.

**12** Attach the upper half of the brace to the back of the swing. Starting on one side, cut two 8" (20.5 cm) pieces of tape. Apply the tape to the top and underside of the brace, as shown, connecting the brace with the upright sidepiece of the back. Be sure to tuck the tape into the corner of the underside of the brace.

**13** Cut three 6" (15 cm) pieces of tape. Wrap them over the tape applied in step 12, where it covers the sidepiece. Stagger the wraps so they extend from the joint to the top of the side piece.

**14** Repeat with the other brace. The seat frame is finished!

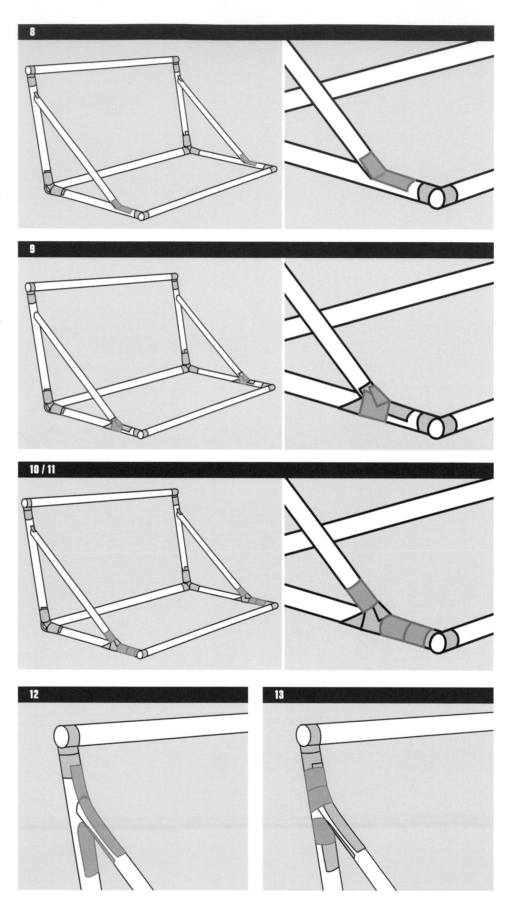

**15** Make the webbing for the seat. Keeping the tape on the roll, attach the end to the back of the seat frame so the tape unrolls under the frame, sticky-side up, as shown. Pull the tape toward the front of the frame.

**16** Wrap the tape around the front of the frame. As you pull the tape toward the back of the frame again, carefully align it with the first pass, and press the two layers of tape together securely. (See the directions for weaving the hammock mesh, pages 86–88, for further details.)

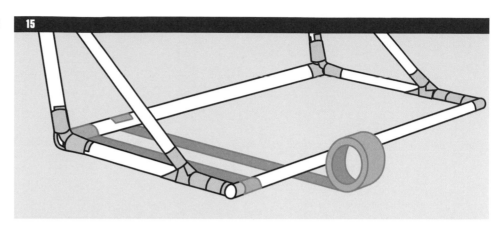

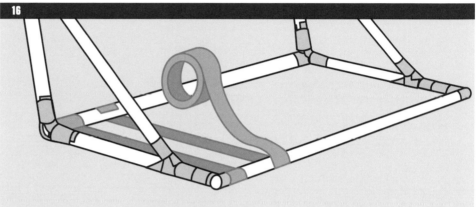

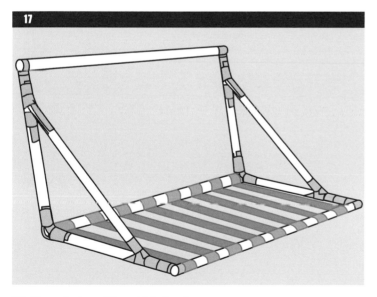

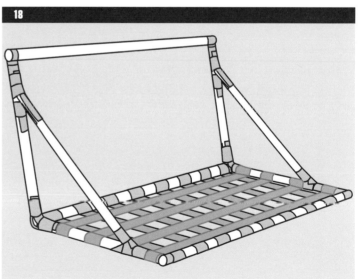

**17** Repeat steps 15 and 16 about every 2" (5 cm) across the seat.

**18** Working from the sides of the seat, repeat steps 16 and 17. The seat webbing is done!

18" [45.5 cm]

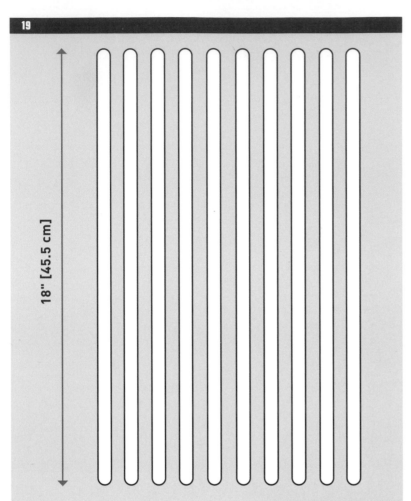

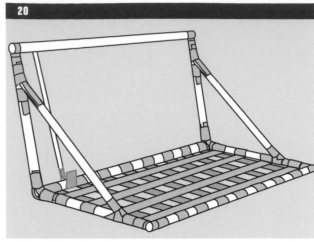

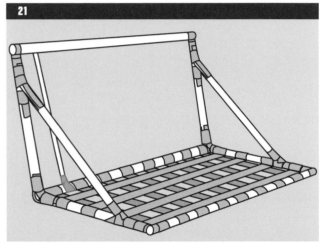

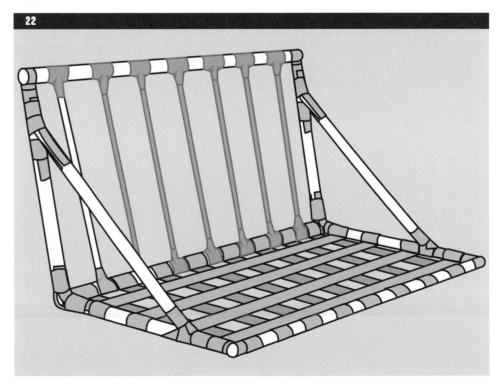

**19** Complete the swing's back. Begin by cutting 18" (45.5 cm) sticks from the ½" (1.3 cm)-thick bamboo garden stakes. These should fit snugly between the upper and lower poles of the back and will be installed between each gap in the seat webbing.

**20** Position the first stick in place about 2½" (6.5 cm) from the side of the frame. Pinch an 8" (20.5 cm) piece of duct tape on one side of the bottom of the stick. Wrap it under the seat frame.

**21** Fold the tape up and pinch the end around the other side of the stick. Repeat steps 20 and 21 at the top of the stick.

**22** Repeat steps 20 through 21 with the other sticks, installing one between each gap in the seat webbing. The seat is done!

**23** Now for the exciting part—bringing the frame and swing together! Place a chair with a comfortable sitting height under the frame. Prop up the front of the chair by about 2" (5 cm). Place the swing seat on top of the chair. This positions the seat at a comfortable height and angle.

**24** Check the position of the swing seat. Reposition the chair, as needed, so the center of the swing seat, running side to side, is directly under the top pole of the frame.

**25** Tie one end of a ball of string around one corner of the swing's back. Pass the string over the top pole of the frame and back to the corresponding corner of the swing's seat. Tie the string in place.

Repeat at the other end of the swing. Use small pieces of tape to attach the string to the top pole to prevent it from sliding. Remove the chair.

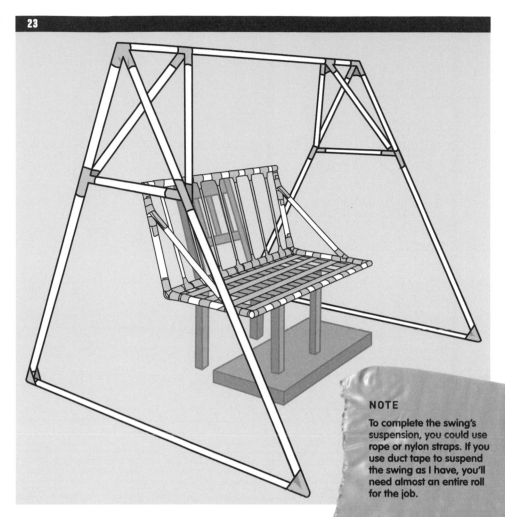

**NOTE**

To complete the swing's suspension, you could use rope or nylon straps. If you use duct tape to suspend the swing as I have, you'll need almost an entire roll for the job.

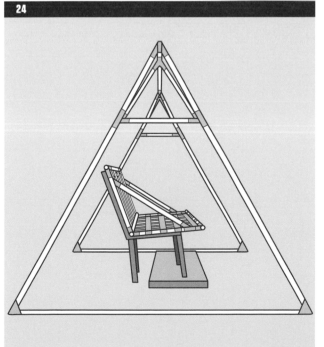

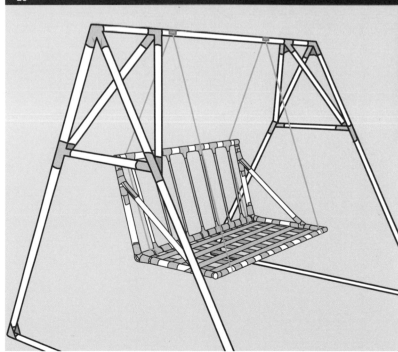

**26** Start at one side of the swing seat, keeping the duct tape on the roll, and attach the end of the tape to the underside of the seat at the back. Unroll the tape under the seat, from back to front. Continue unrolling the tape over the front edge of the seat toward the top pole of the frame, covering the string as you go. Unroll the tape over the top pole, down to the back of the swing seat, and to the underside where you started.

**Important:** Make sure that the suspension is as close as possible to the point where the brace intersects with the top pole. If the suspension is even 5" (13 cm) away from the top pole brace, the top pole may break.

**27** Repeat step 26 four more times, keeping the tape on the roll the entire time.

**28** Repeat steps 26 and 27 at the other end of the swing seat.

**29** At either end of the top pole, place an 8" (20.5 cm) piece of tape over the swing strap to prevent it from slipping.

**30** Cover the sticky side of the swing straps. Carefully align a long piece of tape along the underside of each swing strap and smooth it into place. You're done!

Top the swing off with a couple of cushions, and sit down with a cold drink and a good book.

**NOTE**

The tensile strength of regular duct tape is about 20 lb (9 kg). With a total of twenty layers, the maximum weight limit would be about 400 lb (181 kg)! Using a high-strength tape results in an even stronger swing strap.

**26 / 27 / 28**

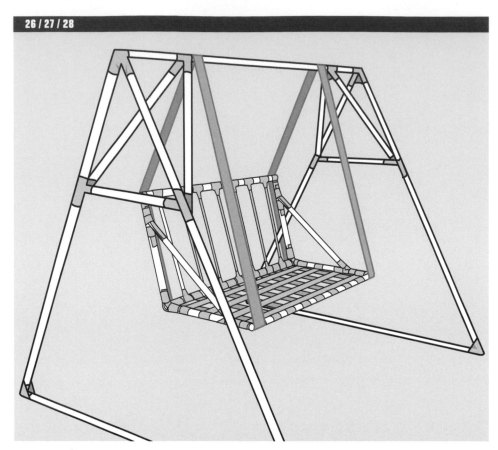

**29**

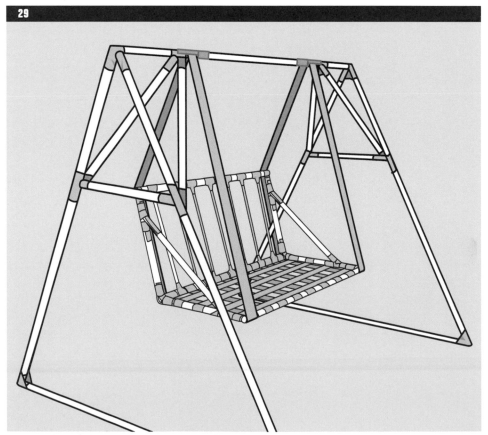

## TESTING! TESTING!

The moment of truth: Will it hold up? If built properly and with the right materials, this design should be able to comfortably support 250 lb (113 kg), and possibly more. However, test the limits of the swing by sitting gingerly on it at first.

Have one person sit on it for an extended period of time—at least thirty minutes—before having two people sit on it at once.

After the first test, inspect all the joints. Look for smeared tape residue, which is evidence the tape is slipping out of place. If you hear any tape ripping or bamboo cracking, carefully get off the seat and make any necessary repairs before trying it again.

## MAINTAINING THE SEAT SWING'S INTEGRITY WHEN NOT IN USE

Duct tape is durable, but it won't last forever. However, you can increase the longevity of the swing by storing it out of direct sunlight and keeping it dry when not in use. Cover the seat swing with a tarp or keep it in a shaded area. Avoid using the swing in temperatures higher than 80°F (26.7°C), because heat weakens the tape's adhesive.

**NOTE**
This design has been tested for a period of six months in relatively mild weather. The seat swing has not been tested in freezing conditions.

If there is one project in this book that will lead your friends and family to realize you're a duct tape genius (and perhaps a little crazy), it's this one. The duct tape kayak is truly an epic project that requires no fewer than twelve rolls of high-quality duct tape to build, as well as—fair warning—a great deal of diligence and determination.

Getting this kayak out on the water, though, and successfully paddling it across a lake may be the pinnacle of any duct tape engineer's career.

**Note:** If built properly and with the right materials, this kayak should hold about 200 lb (91 kg) in still water. Test it in calm, shallow water first.

# KAYAK

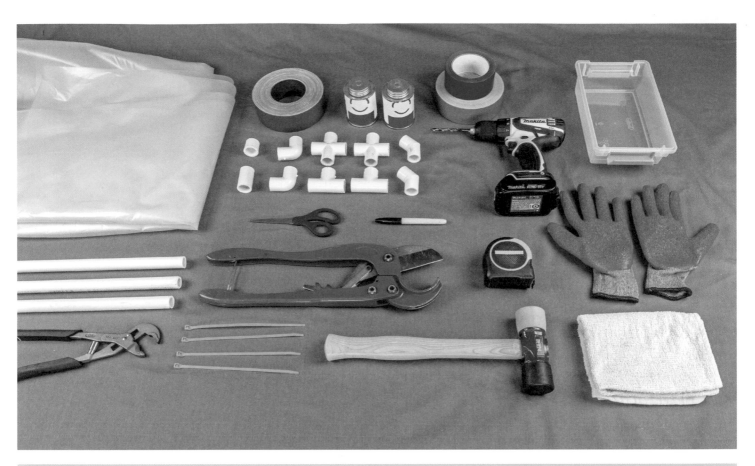

## TOOLS AND MATERIALS

SMALL CONTAINERS FOR ORGANIZING PVC PIPE

TAPE MEASURE

PERMANENT MARKER

PVC PIPE CUTTERS

30' (9.2 M) PLASTIC SHEETING THAT IS 10' (3 M) WIDE AND 6 MIL (25.40 μm) THICK

LATEX OR WATER-RESISTANT GLOVES

MALLET

PIPE PLIERS

PVC PRIMER

PVC SOLVENT WELD

79.25' (24.16 M) OF ½" (1.3 CM) PVC SCHEDULE 40 PIPE

17 ½" (1.3 CM) PVC CROSSES

30 ½" (1.3 CM) PVC TEES

4 ½" (1.3 CM) PVC 90-DEGREE ELBOWS

20 ½" (1.3 CM) PVC 45-DEGREE ELBOWS

4 PVC ½" (1.3 CM) END CAPS

5 ROLLS SHURTECH® BRAND'S T-REX TAPE®

DRILL

¼" (6 MM) DRILL BIT

FOUR (8" [20.5 CM]) CABLE TIES

DRY CLOTH

SCISSORS

7 ROLLS HEAVY-DUTY DUCT TAPE

2 ROLLS COLORED DUCT TAPE (OPTIONAL)

SEVERAL ½" (1.3 CM) PVC COUPLINGS (OPTIONAL)

FOLDING STADIUM SEAT

KAYAK PADDLE

PERSONAL FLOTATION DEVICE

### MATERIAL SUBSTITUTIONS

You can use a fine-tooth saw to cut the PVC, but I strongly recommend PVC pipe cutters. They will save you an enormous amount of time and energy and won't create any PVC dust.

Replace pipe pliers with smaller pliers or vice grips.

You can replace the small hammer with a mallet. Use it gently to avoid breaking the PVC.

*This project uses **ShurTech®** brand's **T-Rex Tape®** for all of the structure and **Duck®** brand's **Max Strength Duck Tape®** for the top layer of the kayak skin.*

## SET UP

**1** To keep the cut PVC pipes sorted, assemble at least fifteen empty boxes and label them according to the pipe lengths in step 2.

**2** Cut the PVC pipe pieces. These are the important structural pieces for the kayak. Write the measurements on them with a permanent marker as you cut them and then place them into the appropriately labeled boxes. You'll need:

| | |
|---|---|
| 1 piece: | 24½" (62 cm) |
| 6 pieces: | 24" (61 cm) |
| 1 piece: | 23½" (59.5 cm) |
| 22 pieces: | 18" (45.5 cm) |
| 1 piece: | 17½" (44.5 cm) |
| 1 piece: | 17" (43 cm) |
| 1 piece: | 16" (40.5 cm) |
| 5 pieces: | 15" (38 cm) |
| 2 pieces: | 12¼" (31 cm) |
| 1 piece: | 12" (30.5 cm) |
| 2 pieces: | 11¼" (28.5 cm) |
| 2 pieces: | 8½" (21.5 cm) |
| 10 pieces: | 6" (15 cm) |
| 14 pieces: | 3" (7.5 cm) |
| 34 pieces: | 1¾" (4.5 cm) |

**3** Put any leftover pieces of PVC and smaller cuts of pipe into a separate box.

**4** Organize the PVC connectors into separate small containers.

**5** Choose a level work surface that is at least 10' × 10' (3 × 3 m). An uneven work surface might result in an uneven kayak. PVC primer stains most surfaces, so cover your work surface with plastic sheeting.

**6** Place the cans of PVC primer and solvent on a scrap piece of cardboard or wood. This prevents the cans from tipping over if the plastic shifts underneath them.

**7** Carefully read the instructions for your PVC primer and cement. Different brands have different cure times and other specific instructions.

**8** Finally, be sure to wear clothes that you don't mind getting stained!

## GET TO WORK

**1** Construct the center strut of the kayak using the specific lengths and connectors shown. Start with the pipe and crosses. Press each cross piece flat against the ground as the solvent cures to ensure the crosses are level, one to the next.

**2** You'll need to work quickly for this step. Glue the 90-degree elbows on the ends. Dry fit a piece of pipe into the elbow before the solvent cures. Use it to check that the connector is pointing straight up.

**3** Glue a 3" (7.5 cm) pipe into the center cross and the one to the right of it. Glue 1¾" (4.5 cm) pieces of pipe into the remaining crosses.

**4** Glue two pairs of pipes and connectors, as shown. Glue them into the 3" (7.5 cm) pipe pieces. These reinforce the kayak's center and provide a stable seating area.

**5** This step is a little tricky. It helps to have a partner hold a 24" (61 cm) length of tape for you as you glue. If you're building solo, place the cut piece of tape somewhere accessible.

Glue the remaining tees onto the 1¾" (4.5 cm) pipe, as shown. While the glue is wet, wrap the connection with the tape, as shown. This prevents the connection from coming undone as the glue cures and helps create the kayak's tapered shape.

**EXTRA MATERIALS FOR FIXING MISTAKES**

Mistakes are inevitable with a big project like this, so purchase extra pipe in case you cut a piece incorrectly. When building the kayak, if you glue the wrong piece into place and it's too long, simply cut it shorter. If it's too short, then use a ½" (1.3 cm) PVC coupling to extend the pipe.

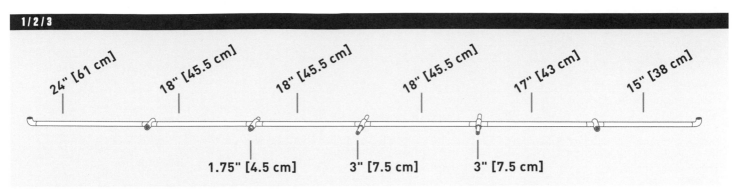

24" [61 cm]    18" [45.5 cm]    18" [45.5 cm]    18" [45.5 cm]    17" [43 cm]    15" [38 cm]

1.75" [4.5 cm]    3" [7.5 cm]    3" [7.5 cm]

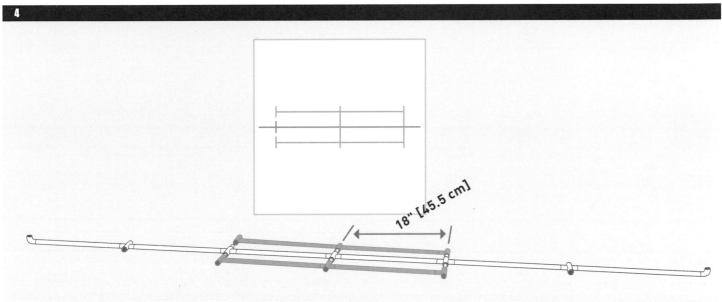

18" [45.5 cm]

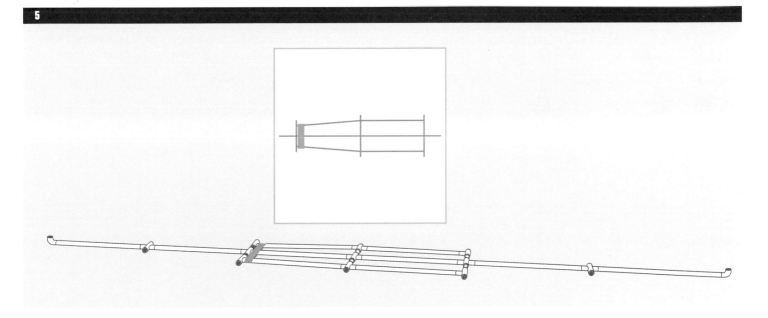

**6** Create the kayak's bow and stern. Glue a 12" (30.5 cm) piece of pipe into the front 90-degree elbow. Glue a 16" (40.5 cm) piece of pipe into the back 90-degree elbow.

Glue the end caps onto the tops of those pipes.

**7** Glue a 1¾" (4.5 cm) pipe into every open tee and cross connection. Glue 45-degree elbows onto each. Glue a 6" (15 cm) pipe into the eight front-most 45-degree elbows.

Glue the two 8½" (21.5 cm) pieces of pipe into the right-most elbows as shown.

**8** As you glue in each 45-degree elbow, dry fit a piece of pipe that's at least 12" (30.5 cm) long. Use the pipe to gauge whether each elbow is perpendicular to the center strut. Adjust the elbows so that they are perpendicular before the glue cures. Remove the dry-fit pipe and use it again for the next elbow.

**9** Create two side struts, as shown. Make sure all crosses are level, one to the next.

**10** Glue the three center-most crosses of one side strut onto the kayak. Repeat on the other side. Wait the minimum curing time before handling. The next step will bend the existing pipe and put tension on the frame, so it's important that the solvent has cured enough to handle the strain.

**11** Get a partner again! Working on both sides of the kayak at once, prime, glue, and affix the back-most crosses at the same time. (It's more difficult to do this one at a time.) Repeat with the front-most crosses.

**12** Glue 45-degree elbows onto each of the crosses. Make sure the open 45-degree elbow connections are pointing straight up.

Glue 6" (15 cm) pieces of pipe into the center 45-degree elbows. In the remaining eight 45-degree elbows, glue a 1¾" (4.5 cm) piece of pipe, a tee, and one 3" (7.5 cm) piece of pipe.

Make sure the side-facing connectors of the tees point toward each other.

**13** Assemble the two top struts separately. Make sure the tees point either straight down or straight across, as shown.

As you build, dry fit pieces of pipe into the open connection of each tee and mark them before you glue them. This helps you see whether the open connections are perfectly square relative to each other.

**6 / 7 / 8**

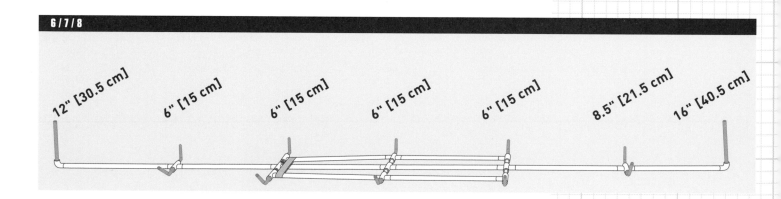

12" [30.5 cm]    6" [15 cm]    6" [15 cm]    6" [15 cm]    6" [15 cm]    8.5" [21.5 cm]    16" [40.5 cm]

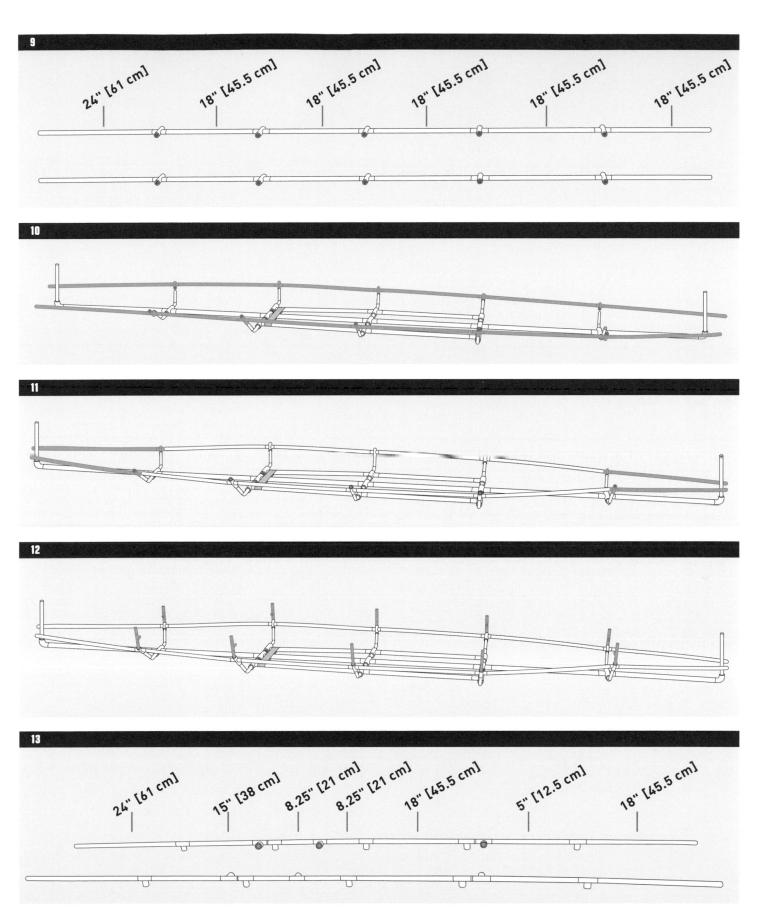

**9**

24" [61 cm]  18" [45.5 cm]  18" [45.5 cm]  18" [45.5 cm]  18" [45.5 cm]  18" [45.5 cm]

**10**

**11**

**12**

**13**

24" [61 cm]  15" [38 cm]  8.25" [21 cm]  8.25" [21 cm]  18" [45.5 cm]  5" [12.5 cm]  18" [45.5 cm]

**14** Following steps 10 and 11, glue the three center-most connections onto the frame, then the back-most pair, and then the front-most. The frame shell is done!

**15** Create two special cross braces by gluing a tee, 3" (7.5 cm) pipe, end cap, and two pieces of pipe, as shown. These will form a tented deck later.

**16** Attach all of the cross braces, as shown. Your frame may have slight variations in width. Dry fit the cross braces before gluing them to make sure they maintain the kayak's tapered shape. Once you confirm the fit, use a mallet to tap one end of the pipe, and then use a pipe wrench to twist and pull the pipe out of the connector.

**17** When you're ready to attach the braces permanently, start by gluing only one end of each brace into place. Then, working from the back toward the front, glue the other end of each brace into its connector. Use a mallet to tap in the pieces firmly into place.

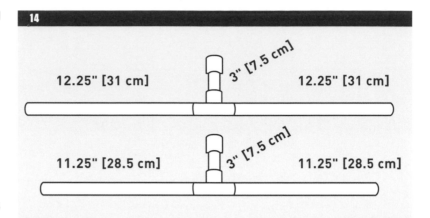

14

12.25" [31 cm]    3" [7.5 cm]    12.25" [31 cm]

11.25" [28.5 cm]    3" [7.5 cm]    11.25" [28.5 cm]

**18** Attach the side struts to the bow and stern of the kayak. Using a ½" (1.3 cm) drill bit, drill a hole through each side strut, about 1" (2.5 cm) from each end. Using the same drill bit, drill one hole through the end cap, and a second hole about 4" (10 cm) from the bottom of the stern. Repeat, drilling through the pipe that forms the kayak's bow. Attach the struts to the bow and stern with cable ties, as shown.

**19** At the bow and stern, wrap tape around the lower left strut, around the upright, and around the lower right strut. Repeat with the upper strut.

**The kayak frame is finished!**

*Before moving on, wait twenty-four hours for the glue to cure fully. Next, test the strength of the frame with a friend by doing the following:*

Position two chairs about 10' (3 m) apart. Rest the bow and stern of the kayak on the chairs so the middle of the frame is suspended above the ground. Have a friend hold one end of the frame to keep it from tipping over.

Climb inside the frame and straddle the three center pipes in the cockpit area. Slowly place more of your body weight onto the frame until your feet are suspended above the ground. If you hear creaking, cracking, or if the frame is deforming significantly, stop. If the frame doesn't do any of those things, it's strong enough to keep you afloat in water!

If you need to strengthen the frame, attach 10' (3 m) pieces of pipe along each of the struts. Place the pipe on the inside of the frame and wrap tape in many places. You could also slide ¼" (0.6 cm) steel rods inside the struts, however these may be expensive and difficult to locate.

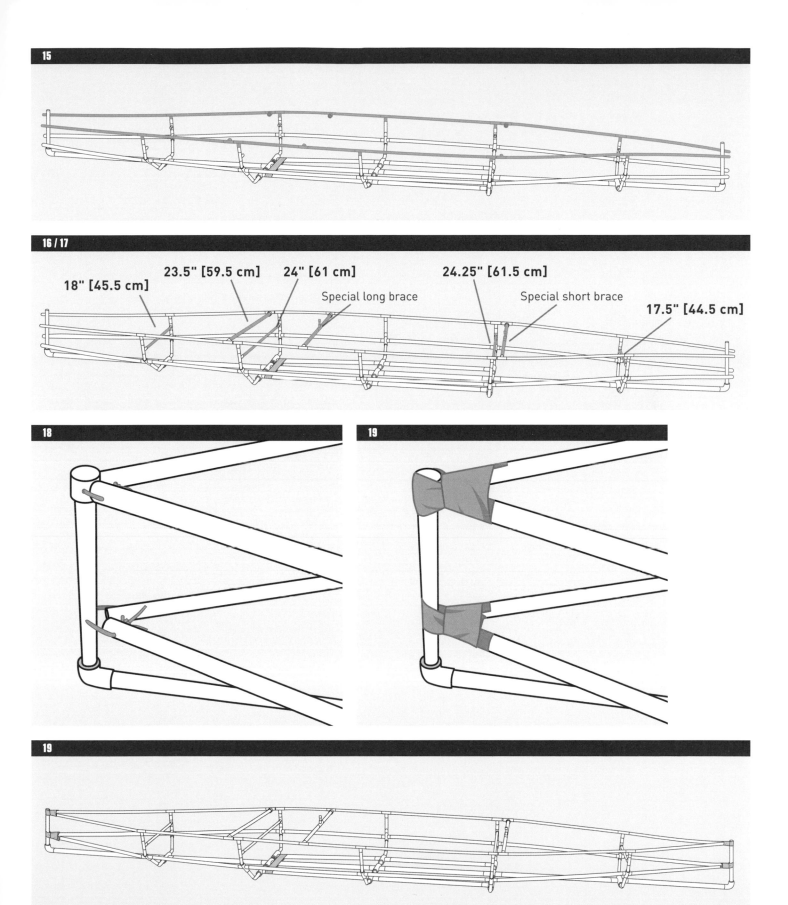

**15**

**16 / 17**

18" [45.5 cm]

23.5" [59.5 cm]

24" [61 cm]

Special long brace

24.25" [61.5 cm]

Special short brace

17.5" [44.5 cm]

**18**

**19**

**19**

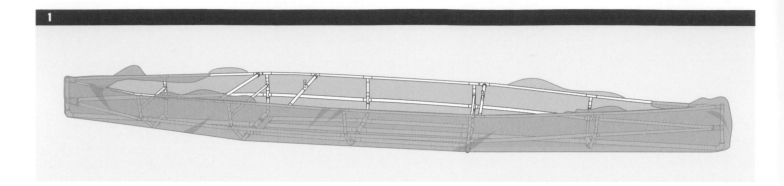

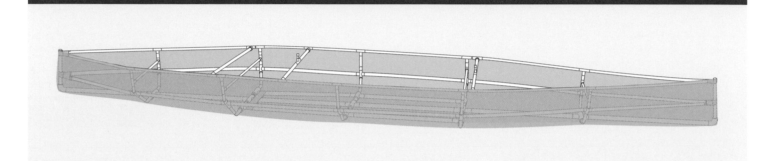

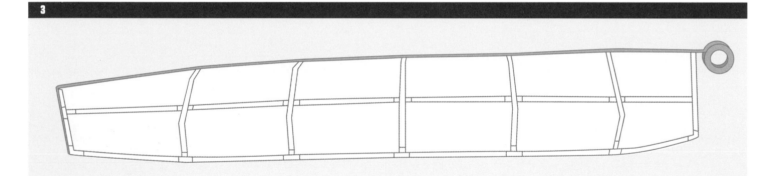

## SKINNING THE KAYAK

**1** Spread out a 10' × 10' (3 × 3 m) sheet of plastic and lay the kayak frame on top. Fold the plastic up along each side of the frame and use scissors to trim the excess. Temporarily tape the plastic in place at each connector.

**2** Now refine the plastic sheeting's fit. Starting at one end of the frame, undo one piece of tape, holding the sheeting in place. Pull the sheeting taut. Cut off the excess so the sheeting reaches just over the top strut. Tape it into place.

Repeat at every connector. Evaluate the sheeting for severe wrinkles and smooth them out by undoing, tightening, and reattaching the plastic sheeting. Small wrinkles are fine, they won't be noticeable once the kayak is covered in tape. Trim the sheeting along the bow and stern so it overlaps by about 1" (2.5 cm).

**3** Get ready to tape. Flip the kayak over and apply a single length of tape along the bow, the bottom, and stern edges of the kayak.

**NOTE**

Although one layer of tape is sufficient, I strongly recommend adding a second layer to guard against tears and leaks. For the top layer, you can use a less expensive tape, such as Max Strength Duck Tape® or Extra Wide Duck Tape®.

**4** Working from the stern of the kayak toward the bow, and working on one side at a time, apply the next long length of duct tape. Overlap the previous piece of tape by half, and unroll the tape 12" to 18" (30.5 to 45.5 cm) at a time. Press the tape down and smooth it as you go.

**5** Continue applying tape along the length of the kayak. The tape will overlap significantly more toward the narrow front (bow) of the kayak. The tape lines will appear to radiate from the bow of the kayak. The goal is to apply the tape so that it will align with the side strut.

**6** Flip the kayak upright and continue applying tape until you reach the top strut. Repeat on the other side.

**7** Cover the bow and stern edges with several layers of tape to cover the loose tape ends and reinforce the seams.

**8** The corners of the 45-degree elbows put extra strain on the plastic sheeting and tape. Reinforce these corners to prevent tearing. Apply at least two layers of tape along each section, as shown.

Tape the top edge of the sheeting to the top strut.

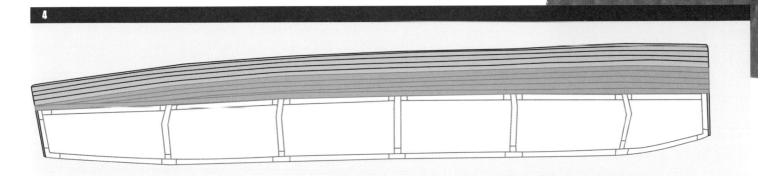

**TIP**
Each time you apply a long strip of tape, use a dry cloth to smooth it and press it into place. This presses out air bubbles and ensures the maximum amount of adhesive comes in contact with the plastic sheeting.

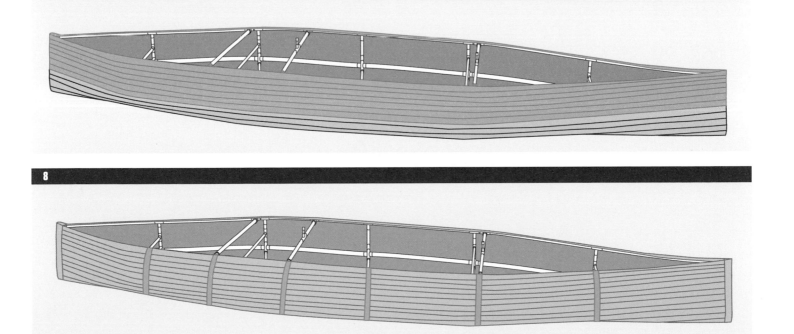

**4**

**5 / 6 / 7**

**8**

**9**_Optional: Cover the cockpit area with a contrasting color of duct tape. Most of the frame won't be visible under the deck, so it's really not necessary to tape it at all.

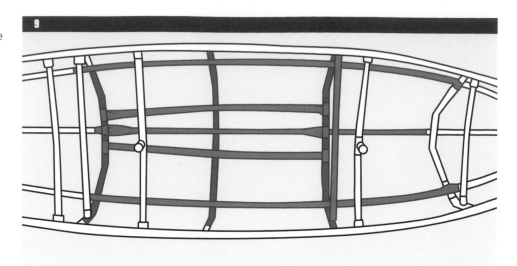

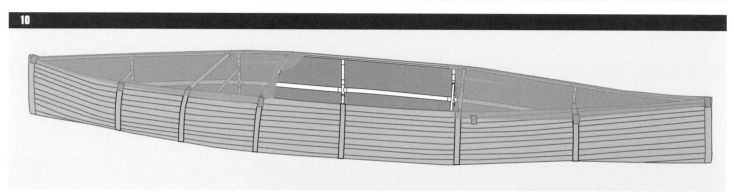

**10**_Create the deck. Cut a piece of plastic sheeting that fits over the top of the kayak at the bow and stern, as shown. Temporarily tape the sheeting in place. Then fit it, as in step 2, alternating between pulling the sheet taut, trimming it with scissors, and applying a small piece of tape to keep it in place.

**11**_At the high point, at the center of the bow's cockpit edge, cut the plastic along the midline and overlap the edges, as shown, to take out excess wrinkling. Tape the cut edges.

**12**_Apply a single long piece of tape that pulls the sheeting taut and attaches it to the cockpit edge.

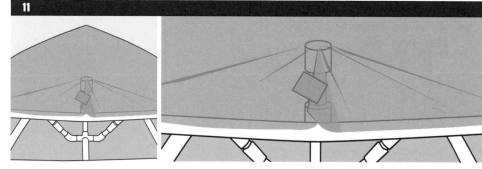

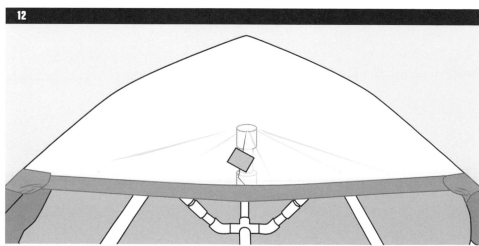

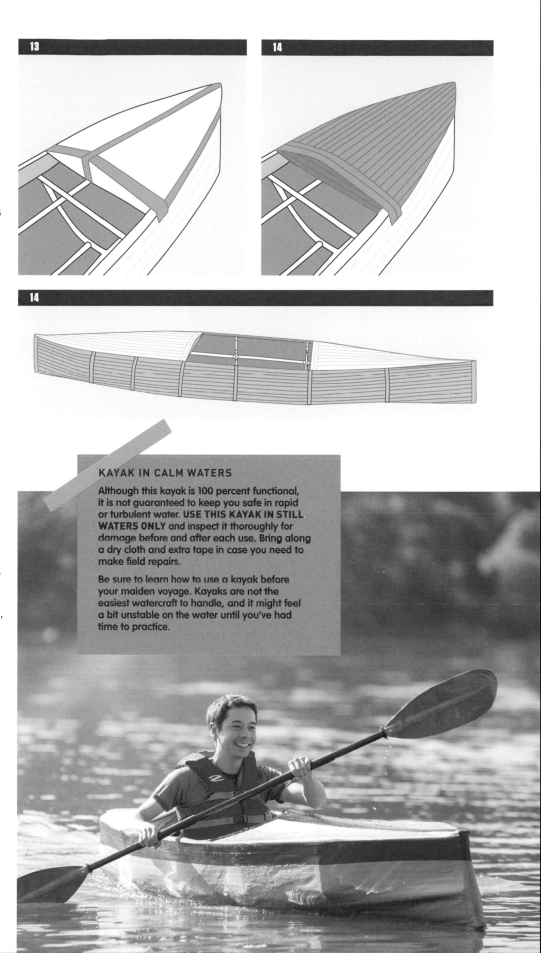

**13** Apply at least two layers of tape very tightly over the high point, above the cross beam. Next apply another two layers of tape that reach from the underside of the cross beam to the tip of the frame. The tape will be more taut than the sheeting. Press the tape onto the sheeting to lift it up. These lengths of tape help the sheeting keep its shape as you cover it with tape, and ensure it retains the graceful curve that will prevent water from pooling on the deck.

**14** Lay overlapping pieces of tape along the sheeting toward the kayak's bow. Next apply horizontal strips of tape to the sheeting that faces the cockpit. Avoid wrapping tape from the underside of the cross beam toward the tip of the kayak. This may cause the plastic to lose tension and create pockets for water to pool in.

Repeat steps 11 through 14 at the kayak's stern.

The kayak is complete! For a cockpit seat, tape a folding stadium seat to the kayak frame, or build your own out of PVC, foam, and tape. Decorate it with colored tape or permanent marker decals. Create waterproof pockets for storing your phone, or build elastic tie-downs for holding your bag securely as you paddle.

**KAYAK IN CALM WATERS**

Although this kayak is 100 percent functional, it is not guaranteed to keep you safe in rapid or turbulent water. **USE THIS KAYAK IN STILL WATERS ONLY** and inspect it thoroughly for damage before and after each use. Bring along a dry cloth and extra tape in case you need to make field repairs.

Be sure to learn how to use a kayak before your maiden voyage. Kayaks are not the easiest watercraft to handle, and it might feel a bit unstable on the water until you've had time to practice.

# 4

# BAL

Stand clear! Get ready to launch tennis balls and paper rockets with contraptions held together with durable duct tape. If flinging water balloons from a giant slingshot or shooting a sci-fi launcher is what gets you fired up, these projects are meant for you. Be forewarned: They may shoot farther than you think!

LISTICS

In my earlier book, *Rubber Band Engineer*, I claim it is possible to scale up my tabletop pyramid catapult to a full-blown "war" machine. This design achieves that goal and includes a few extra features to make it even more functional. But look out—the giant pyramid catapult can easily fling a tennis ball across a wide street and into your neighbor's yard. (I know from experience!)

# GIANT PYRAMID CATAPULT

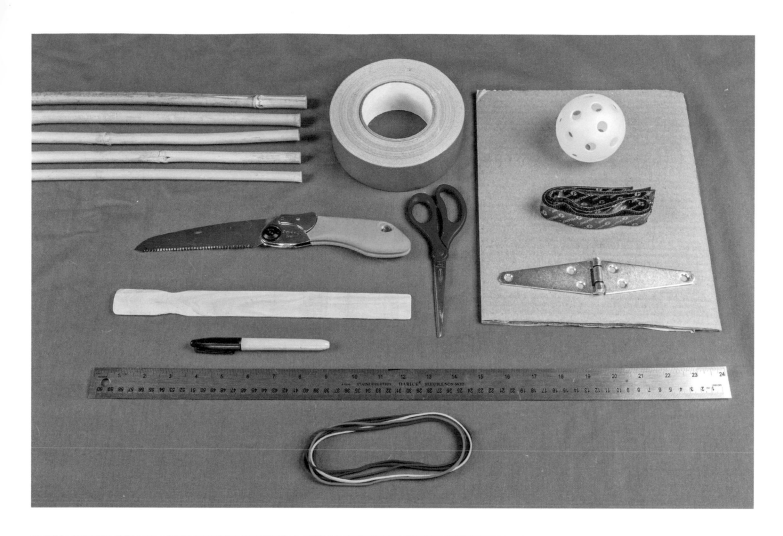

## TOOLS AND MATERIALS

**9 BAMBOO GARDEN POLES, AT LEAST 6' (1.8 M) LONG AND ½" (1.3 CM) WIDE**

**METAL RULER**

**PERMANENT MARKER**

**FINE-TOOTH SAW OR HEAVY-DUTY GARDEN LOPPERS WITH A CURVED BLADE**

**8 YARDS (7.5 M) HEAVY-DUTY DUCT TAPE**

**9 YARDS (8.25 M) CONTRASTING COLOR DUCT TAPE (OPTIONAL)**

**4" (10 CM) STRAP HINGE**

**5 (OR MORE) 7" (18 CM) RUBBER BANDS**

**SCISSORS**

**10" (25.5 CM) HOOK AND LOOP FASTENERS (SUCH AS VELCRO)**

**CARDBOARD**

**1 PAINT STIRRER**

**PLASTIC BALL, TENNIS BALL, OR OTHER PROJECTILE**

## MATERIAL SUBSTITUTIONS

You can use thick plastic garden stakes, ½" (1.3 cm) PVC pipe, or any other long, rigid material that can be cut, instead of bamboo poles.

*This project uses **Duck**® brand's **Max Strength Duck Tape**® and **Color Duck Tape**® in red and yellow.*

**1** Select the thickest and straightest bamboo sticks. Cut four of them to 48" (122 cm) and two of them to 44" (112 cm).

Create two triangles out of the sticks using the corner connection technique on page 95. One side in each triangle is shorter than the other two. This allows the catapult's throwing arm to fire at a higher angle. It also makes it easier to reach the throwing arm from a crouching position when you're ready to fire.

**2** Hold the two triangles together along a long side. Make sure they match up evenly, especially at the base. Tape them together in at least five places. This joined edge is the front of the catapult. Set up the joined triangles as a catapult frame. The other long side is against the ground, and the short side is upright.

**3** Cut one more bamboo stick to 36" (91.5 cm). This is the third side of the frame base. Begin taping it to the frame at one corner by laying an 8" (20.5 cm) strip of duct tape underneath.

**4** Wrap the tape around the corner, as shown. Press a second 6" (15 cm) piece of tape over the first.

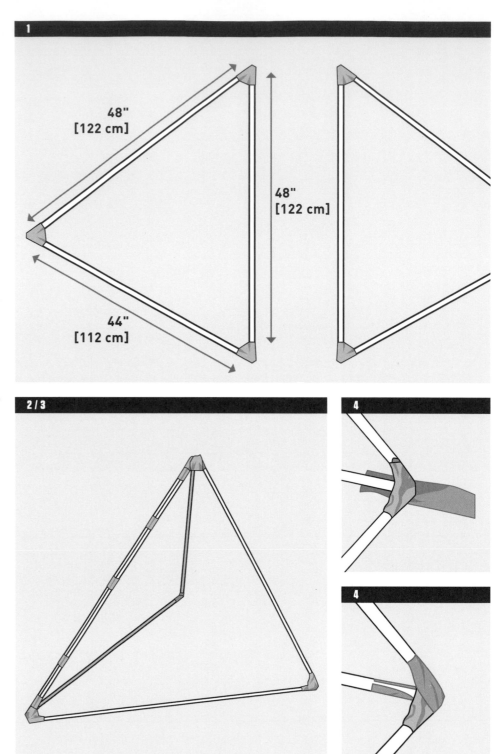

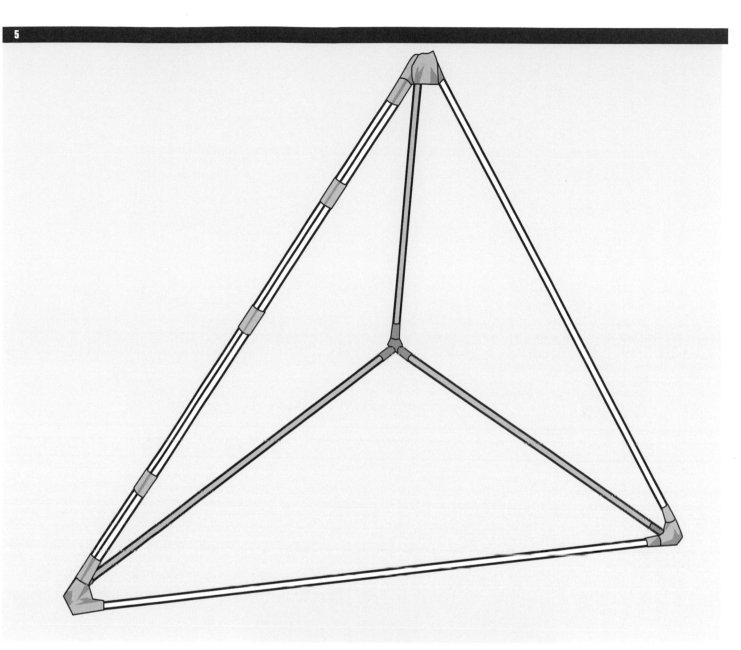

**5**_Wrap tape around all three sticks to prevent the first layers of tape from peeling up over time. Repeat on the other side to complete the pyramid frame.

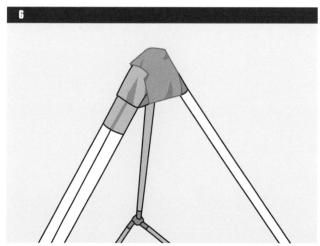

**6**_Reinforce the apex of the pyramid by wrapping several layers of duct tape over and under it. Make sure it is secure: The catapult's throwing arm will collide with this part of the frame, and will, eventually, tear it apart if the joint is not strong.

**7**_Make the catapult's throwing arm. Select two more straight bamboo sticks of equal diameter. Cut them to 56" (142 cm). Lay the sticks side by side. Tape them together tightly in five places, equally spaced.

**8**_Lay one flange of the hinge at one end of the throwing arm. Make sure the hinge knuckles face upward.

**9**_Wrap duct tape tightly around the hinge, covering it completely. Don't tape over the knuckles.

**10**_Position the hinge's other flange against the inside front edge of the pyramid frame. Make sure the hinge is positioned flat against the pair of sticks. Wrap duct tape tightly around the flange and the bamboo, making sure to leave the knuckles exposed.

**11**_Lift the free end of the throwing arm. Loop at least five 7" (18 cm) rubber bands around the throwing arm and the apex of the frame.

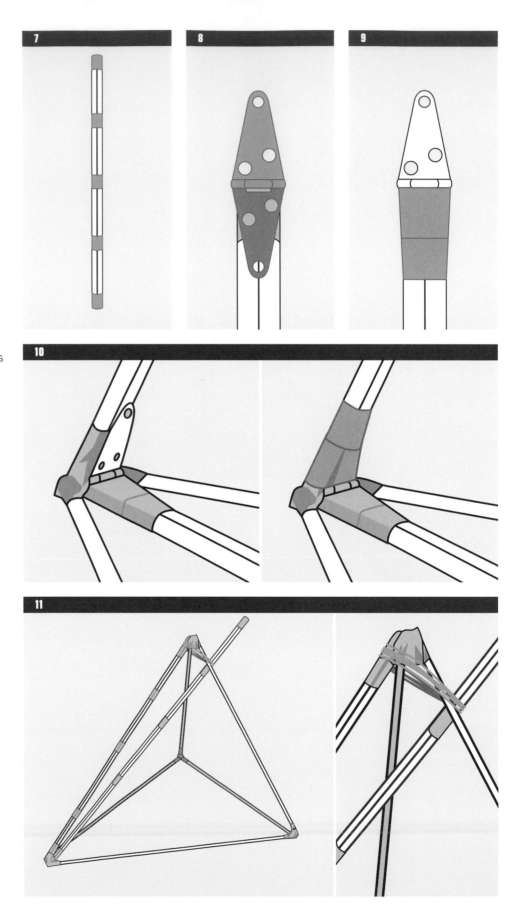

**12** Create a strap to hold the rubber bands in place. Fold a 5" (12.5 cm) piece of tape in half lengthwise—this is the strap. Apply one piece of adhesive-backed hook and loop fastener (such as Velcro) to the frame's apex, and the other piece to the underside of one end of the strap. Connect the two pieces of fastener.

Tape the opposite end of the strap to the front of the catapult frame, wrapping them together securely. This prevents the rubber bands from coming undone during use, and allows you to add and remove bands easily to find the perfect amount of firepower.

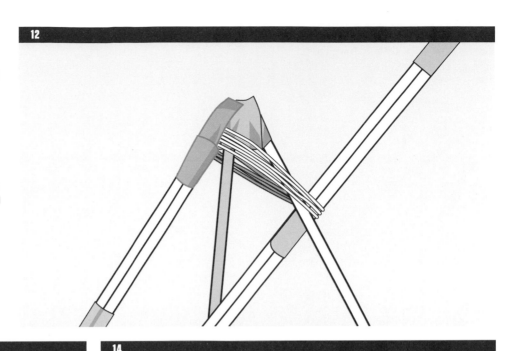

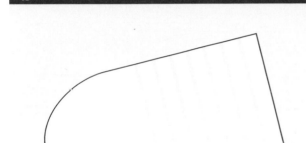

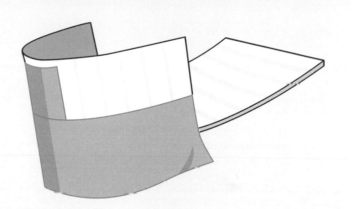

**13** Make the catapult bucket for holding the projectile. Cut a 5" × 4" (12.5 × 10 cm) cardboard rectangle. Round the corners at one end.

**14** Cut a 9" × 2" (23 × 5 cm) piece of cardboard with the corrugations running crosswise. Roll the strip to shape it. Wrap it around the rounded end of the cardboard and tape it in place. The tape should extend all the way around the curve.

**15** Flip the bucket over. Cut slots into the tape to create tabs as shown. Fold the tabs down one by one.

**16** Cover the entire bucket with tape. Curl the squared end upward.

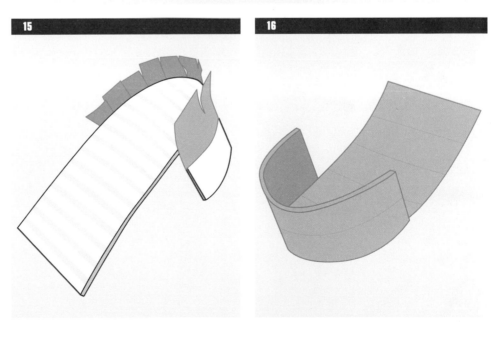

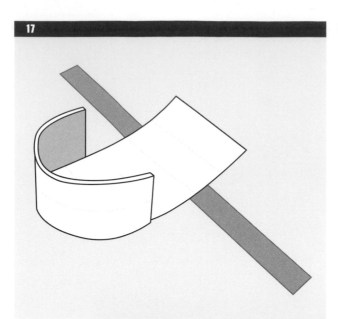

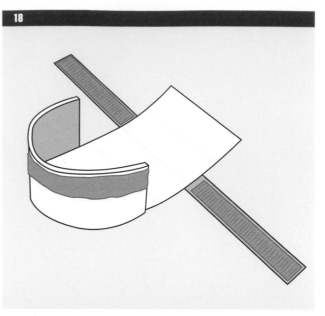

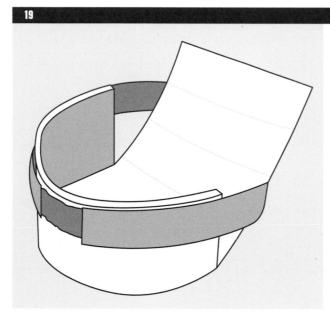

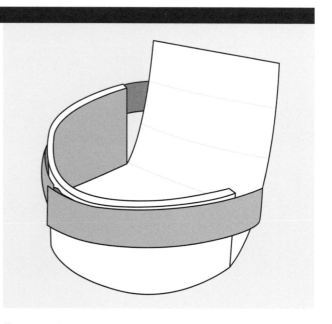

**17** Fold a 14" (35.5 cm) piece of tape in half lengthwise so that it sticks to itself. Tape it to the back of the bucket, as shown, with another piece of tape.

**18** Apply a 9" (23 cm) hook and loop fastener along the front of the bucket and two 4" (10 cm) hook and loop fasteners on each of the straps.

**19** The position of the straps allows you to change the catapult's trajectory:

*Loosening the straps* tilts the bucket backward. This causes the projectile to be flung upward at a higher trajectory.

*Tightening the straps* pulls the back of the bucket into an upright position, which causes the projectile to launch forward in a straighter trajectory.

**20** The bucket will be exposed to intense bursts of force, which may destabilize it. To prevent this, build a bucket support platform. Tape a 4" (10 cm) piece of paint stirrer crosswise about 3" (7.5 cm) from the end of the throwing arm. Wrap the tape tightly around the paint stirrer.

**21** Press another piece of tape over the paint stirrer, along the throwing arm. Tightly wrap two more pieces of tape around the throwing arm on either side of the paint stirrer.

**22** Looking from underneath the throwing arm: Position the bucket on top of the support platform and attach it with two pieces of duct tape.

**23** Wrap two more pieces of tape, as shown. These pieces extend up the sides of the bucket.

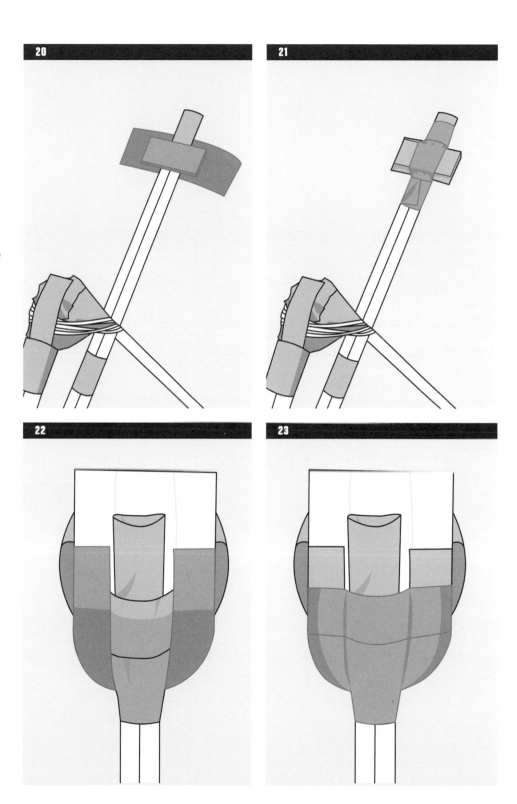

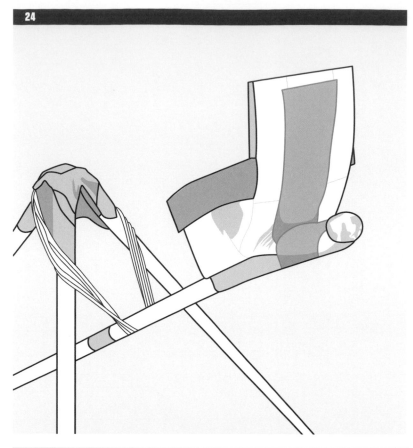

**24** Press a final piece of tape into the corner between the back of the bucket and the end of the throwing arm. Wrap the end of the throwing arm with tape.

**25** Create a handle for the throwing arm. Layer three 6" (15 cm) pieces of tape evenly. Attach one end of the layered tape to the end of the throwing arm. Fold the tape hanging off the end in half, so it sticks to itself. Wrap another piece of tape around the end of the throwing arm to keep the handle in place.

***The giant catapult is complete!***
Decorate the catapult with colored or patterned tape, if you choose. Grab a tennis or plastic ball and head outside.

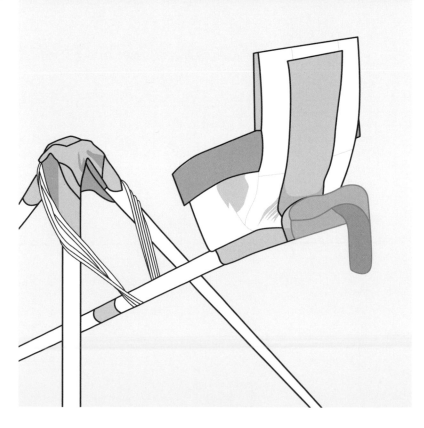

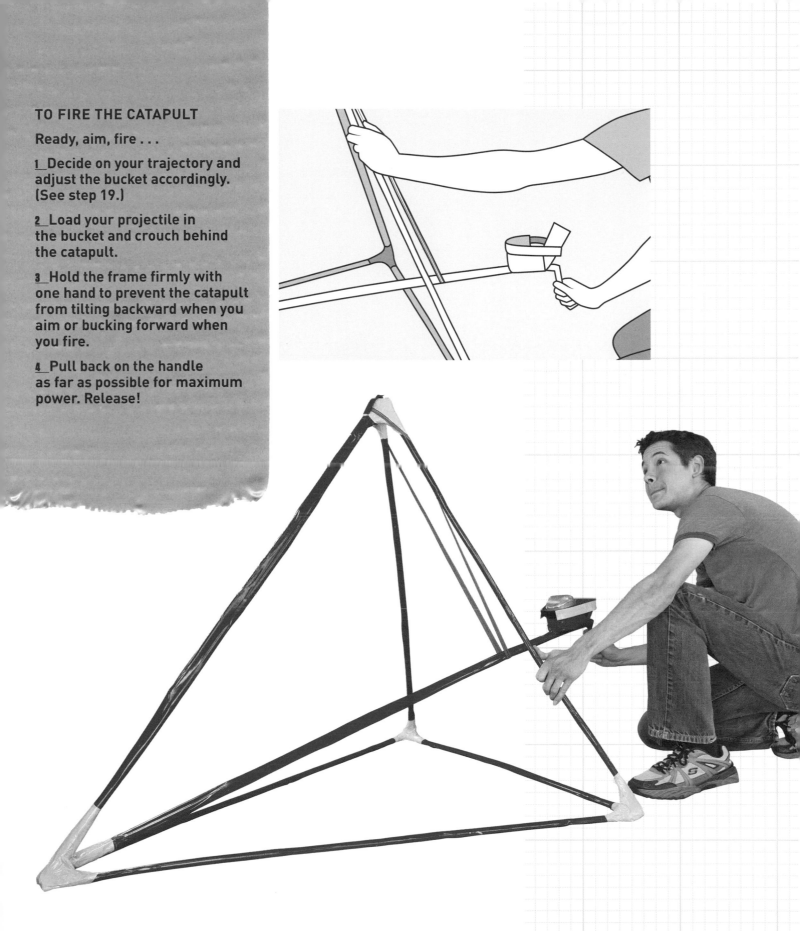

## TO FIRE THE CATAPULT

**Ready, aim, fire . . .**

**1_** Decide on your trajectory and adjust the bucket accordingly. (See step 19.)

**2_** Load your projectile in the bucket and crouch behind the catapult.

**3_** Hold the frame firmly with one hand to prevent the catapult from tilting backward when you aim or bucking forward when you fire.

**4_** Pull back on the handle as far as possible for maximum power. Release!

This contraption is super easy to build, yet incredibly durable and high performing. Launch projectiles 50' (15.25 m), or farther, with consistent power and accuracy. Then help a friend build one and let the games begin!

# GIANT SLINGSHOT

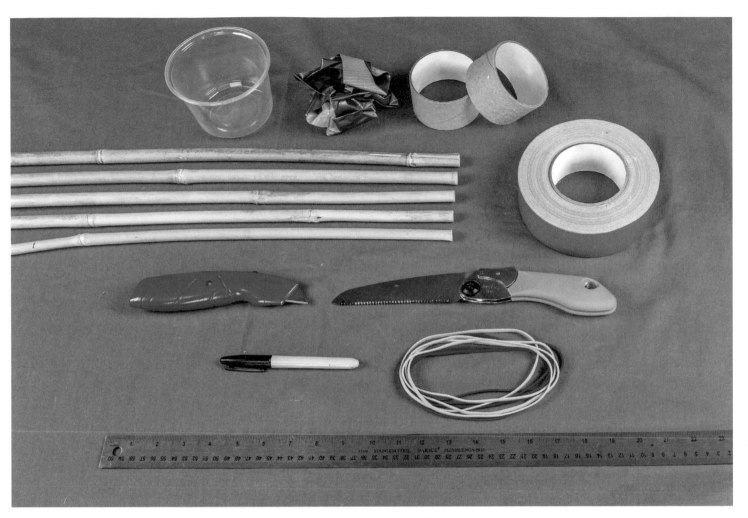

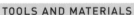

## TOOLS AND MATERIALS

5 BAMBOO GARDEN STAKES, 6' (91.8 M) LONG

FINE-TOOTH SAW OR OTHER BAMBOO CUTTING TOOL

METAL RULER

PERMANENT MARKER

4 YARDS (3.65 M) HEAVY-DUTY DUCT TAPE

EIGHT 7" (18 CM) RUBBER BANDS

16 OZ (500 ML) PLASTIC DELI CONTAINER

SCRAP PIECES OF DUCT TAPE

2 EMPTY DUCT TAPE ROLLS

UTILITY KNIFE

## MATERIAL SUBSTITUTIONS

You can use a ¾" (2 cm) schedule 40 PVC pipe instead of bamboo garden stakes.

I've used scrap tape and empty rolls to make a duct tape–based projectile, but you can try launching anything about the size of a tennis ball.

You can use any durable container that can hold a tennis ball–size object instead of a deli container.

*This project uses **Duck**® brand's*
**Max Strength Duck Tape**®

**1**__Cut the bamboo stakes into five 48"
(122 cm) pieces and two 24" (61 cm)
pieces. Don't worry if the ends splinter
a bit; they'll be wrapped in tape later.

**2**__Use the corner-connection technique
shown on page 95 to form an equilateral
triangle using three 48" (122 cm) pieces.
Wrap the connections tightly, pressing
down on the duct tape to secure it. Consider using two layers of tape because
this structure will be under stress when
you pull back on the sling.

**3**__Place a 10" (25.5 cm) length of tape
sticky-side up under one corner of the
triangle and position a fourth 48" (122 cm)
stake on top.

**4**__Fold the duct tape tightly over the
corner so it sandwiches the fourth stake
and adheres to itself. Wrap a 6" (15 cm)
piece of tape around the new join connection for a cleaner look.

**5** Repeat step 4 on a second corner of the triangle. Connect the fourth and fifth stakes together with another V connection.

**6** Use the overlap-connection technique, shown on page 95, to attach the two 24" (61 cm) pieces. These support the upper triangle and act as foot braces when firing the slingshot. The position of the supports affects the angle of the upper triangle, which, in turn, affects the angle at which the slingshot shoots.

For example, if the upright triangle is at a 90-degree angle, then the slingshot will fire straight forward. Here, the slingshot is designed to shoot upward at about a 40-degree angle. To achieve this, the bottom of each 24" (61 cm) support piece is taped at the middle of the sides of the lower triangle at a right angle. The top of the support is taped where it intersects with the upper triangle.

**7** Center two rubber bands concentrically under one side of the frame.

**8** Pull one end of the stacked bands through the other and tighten.

**9** Repeat step 8 on all three sides of the slingshot and at the apex of the structure. The pair of rubber bands at the apex add extra power and elevates the sling to a height that is comfortable to grasp.

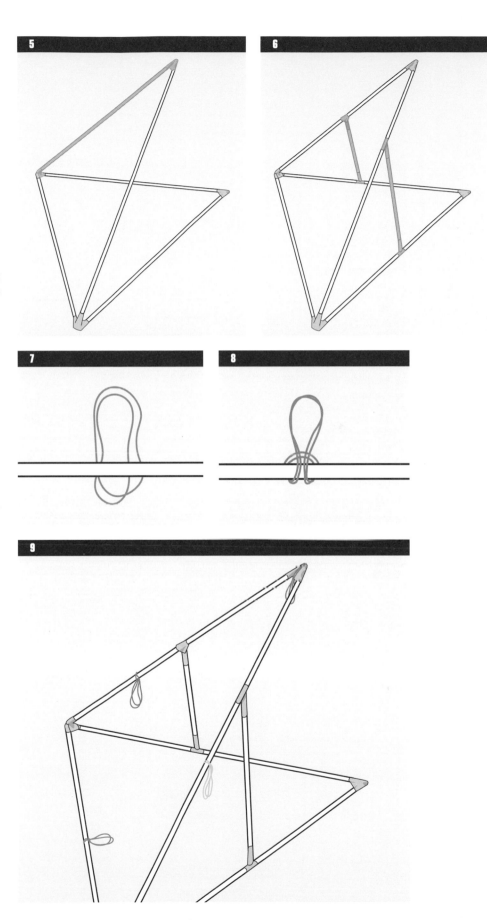

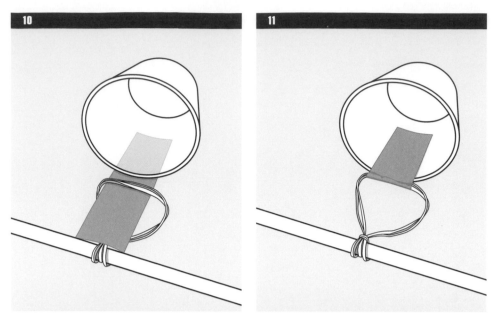

**10** Attach the sling. Apply an 8" (20.5 cm) piece of duct tape to the deli container so that half the tape's length is on the container's outside. Position the taped edge, sticky-side up, so it wraps through one pair of rubber bands.

**11** Fold the duct tape over the rubber bands and firmly apply it to the inside of the container.

**12** Repeat with the other three pairs of rubber bands. This process can be a little tricky to do alone. Have a friend hold the rubber bands in place while you wrap the tape over the edge of the sling.

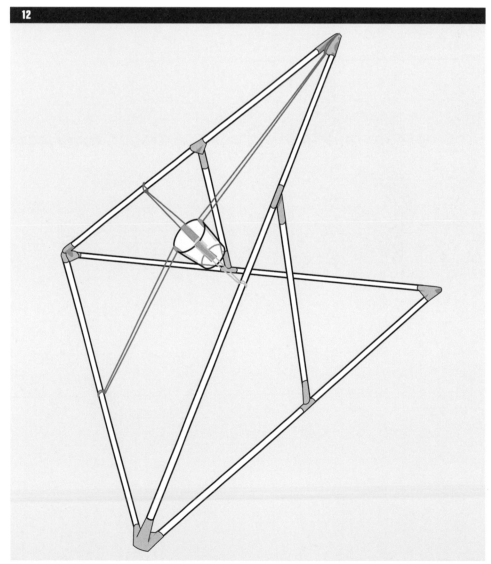

**13** The tension of the rubber bands will pull on the tape and cause it to bunch up and wrinkle. Eventually it may come undone. Prevent this by wrapping a long piece of tape around the top outside edge of the container. If desired, cut short vertical slits in the tape, so that it lies flat on the angled sides of the container when you wrap it.

**14** Create a handle for the slingshot. Center a 6" (15 cm) length of duct tape on a 10" (25.5 cm) piece of tape, sticky sides together. Leave the 2" (5 cm) adhesive ends exposed.

**15** Attach the adhesive ends of the handle to the lower sides of the container. As in step 13, secure the ends by wrapping a length of tape around the lower outside edge of the container. Make short cuts in the tape, as desired, to help it lie flat. Your giant slingshot is complete!

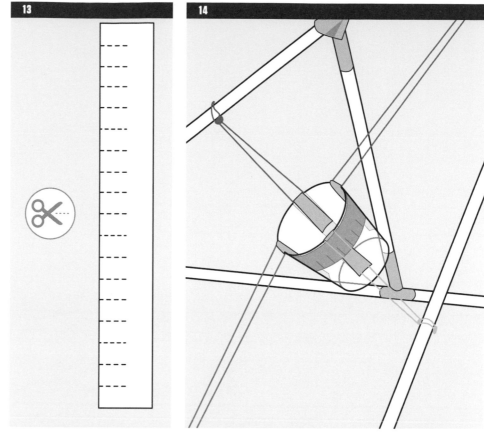

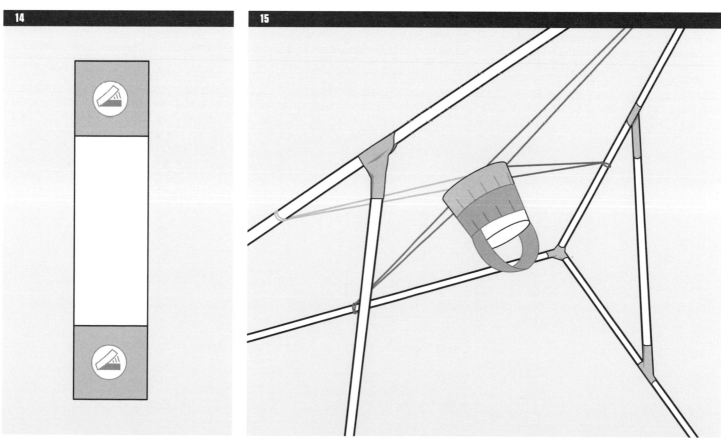

**16**  Make a projectile. Rather than throw your scraps of duct tape and empty tape rolls away, do a little creative recycling and turn them into a projectile for your slingshot. Gather tape scraps and tightly wad them into a ball to fit inside a tape roll. If needed, wrap tape around the ball to hold it together.

**17**  Use the utility knife to cut a ¾" (2 cm) segment from an empty tape roll.

**18**  Wrap a piece of tape around the tape roll, tightening it to close the gap and make the tape roll slightly smaller in diameter. Place the scrap ball inside the roll.

**19**  Wedge the modified tape roll, sideways, into the center of another empty roll; it should fit snugly.

**20**  Carefully wrap the two rolls in duct tape, covering all cardboard surfaces. This reduces air resistance. This projectile will be dense enough to travel a satisfying distance, but safe enough that you won't break a window!

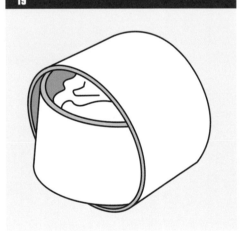

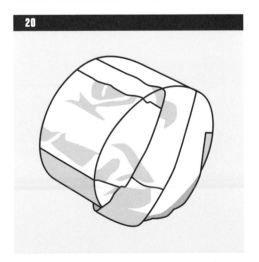

## DESIGN VARIABLES

You can vary the proportions of this design scale easily. You can make a slingshot that is 6" or 6' (15 cm or 1.8 m) tall! Keep in mind that larger structures may require more support pieces or stronger materials. Try adding more rubber bands for even greater range!

## LAUNCHING YOUR SLINGSHOT

Be judicious about your target.

1_ Load and aim the slingshot.

2_ Sit on the ground behind the slingshot and brace your feet against the upright support pieces.

3_ Grab the handle. Pull down and back and then quickly release!

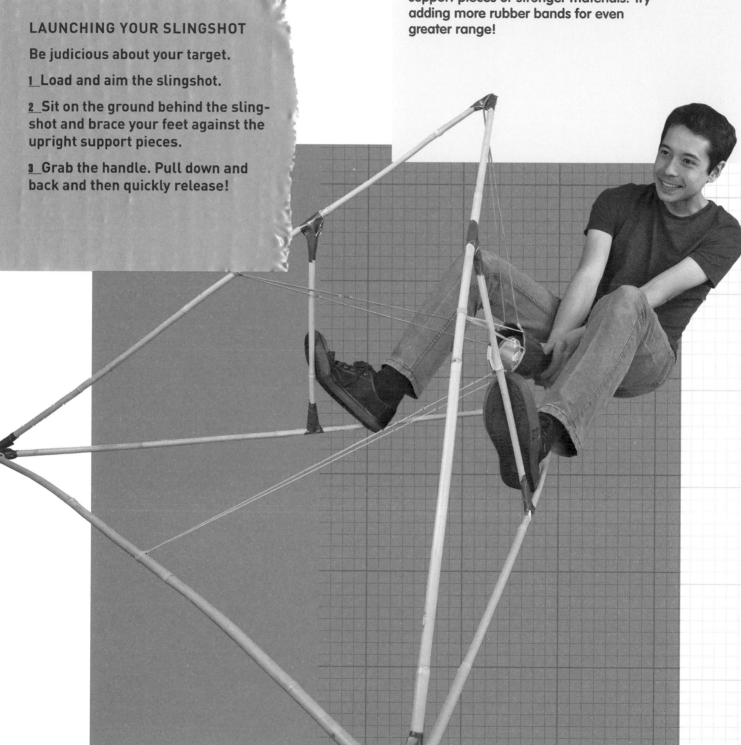

Portable, powerful, and built like a prop from a sci-fi film, this rocket launcher transcends the genre of air-powered cannons. With the push of a button, you can easily launch your rockets more than 100' (30.5 m), proving this design is as effective as it looks.

# ROCKET LAUNCHER

## MATERIAL SUBSTITUTIONS

You can use two ½" (1.3 cm) elbow connectors instead of flexible PVC coupling, or search online for directions on how to bend normal PVC pipe using a blow dryer and sand.

Instead of a sprinkler valve and electronics, you can use a PVC ball valve, but it will be more challenging to release the stored air pressure rapidly.

## TOOLS AND MATERIALS

**FOR THE LAUNCHER:**

PVC PIPE CUTTERS

METAL RULER

10" (25.5 CM) OF 2" (5 CM)-WIDE PVC PIPE

36" (91.5 CM) OF ½" (1.3 CM)-WIDE PVC PIPE

2 (2" [5 CM]) PVC END CAPS

2" (5 CM) PVC COUPLER

2" TO ½" (5 TO 1.3 CM) PVC REDUCER

PVC PRIMER AND SOLVENT WELD

2" (5 CM) PVC TEE

½" × 18" (1.3 × 45.5 CM) FLEXIBLE PVC REPAIR COUPLING

3 YARDS (2.75 M) HEAVY-DUTY DUCT TAPE

UTILITY KNIFE

DRILL

DRILL BIT SLIGHTLY WIDER THAN THE TIRE VALVE

INNER-MOUNTED TIRE VALVE WITH SCHRADER STEM

TWO ½" TO ¾" (1.3 TO 2 CM) PVC THREADED REDUCERS

¾" (2 CM) INLINE ELECTRONIC SPRINKLER VALVE

THREAD SEAL TAPE

WIRE STRIPPERS

9-VOLT BATTERY

9-VOLT BATTERY CLIP WITH WIRE LEADS

MOMENTARY PUSH-BUTTON SWITCH WITH LEADS

HANDHELD AIR PUMP

**FOR THE ROCKET:**

1 YARD (1 M) REGULAR DUCT TAPE

2 SHEETS 8½" × 11" (21.5 × 28 CM) CARD STOCK

SCRAP PIECE ½" (1.3 CM) PVC PIPE, AT LEAST 10" (25.5 CM) LONG

SCISSORS

**FOR DECORATIVE MATERIALS:** (OPTIONAL)

2 YARDS (2 M) DECORATIVE TAPE

BLACK SPRAY PAINT

RED ACRYLIC PAINT

*This project uses **Duck**® brand's **Max Strength Duck Tape**® and **Color Duck Tape**® in black and red.*

## MAKE THE LAUNCHER

**1** Arrange the pressure-chamber pieces, as shown. Cut a 10" (25.5 cm) piece of the 2" (5 cm) PVC pipe.

Test fit the end cap, 10" (25.5 cm) pipe, and coupler. Cut a 1¾" (4.5 cm) piece of ½" (1.3 cm) PVC pipe. Test fit the 2" to ½" (5 to 1.3 cm) PVC reducer, the 1¾" (4.5 cm) piece of pipe, and the ½" to ¾" (1.3 to 2 cm) PVC reducer.

**2** Glue the pieces together using PVC primer and solvent weld, as shown. Follow the manufacturer's instructions when using solvent weld compounds. For now, do not glue the pressure chamber to the reducer.

Spray paint the sprinkler valve attachment, if desired.

**3** Drill a hole through the pressure chamber at the point where the coupler and pipe overlap. The hole should be slightly larger than the diameter of the tire valve.

**4** Insert the valve from the inside of the pressure chamber so the threaded stem is exposed. Tighten the nut with pliers until the rubber washer is pressed firmly against the inside of the pressure chamber wall.

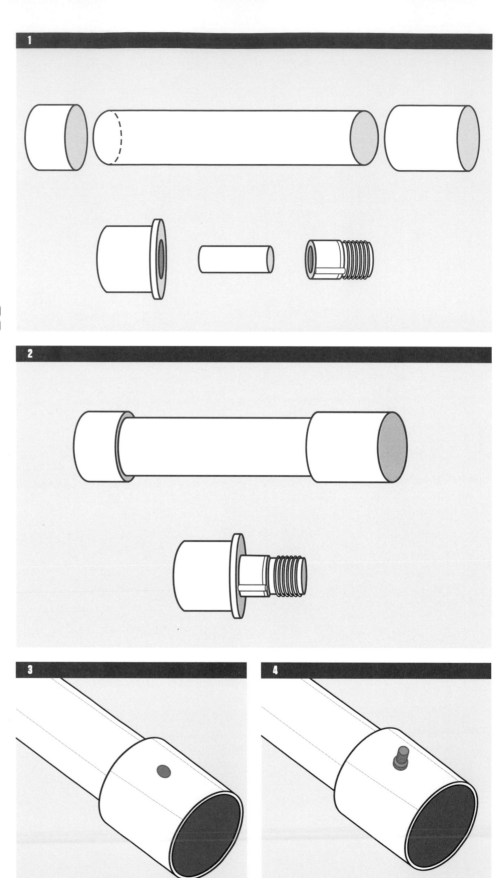

**5**_Test the valve seal. Dry fit the 2" to ½" (5 to 1.3 cm) PVC reducer, 1½" (4 cm) piece of ½" (1.3 cm) pipe, and one ½" to ¾" (1.3 to 2 cm) PVC threaded reducer onto the open end of the coupler.

Partially screw the pressure chamber onto the sprinkler valve. Pump a few PSI into the pressure chamber to ensure the valve is working correctly and that there are no obvious air leaks.

Release the air pressure, detach the sprinkler attachment, and unscrew the sprinkler valve.

Disassemble the pieces and glue them back together.

**6**_This launcher is designed to be used at relatively low pressure. Protect yourself from PVC shrapnel by covering the pressure chamber lengthwise with pieces of heavy-duty duct tape, leaving about 3" (7.5 cm) hanging off the side with the end cap.

**7**_Cut all loose tape strips down the center. Pull on the tabs as you apply the tape over the top of the end cap.

Repeat these steps one more time to further protect yourself from an exploding pressure chamber.

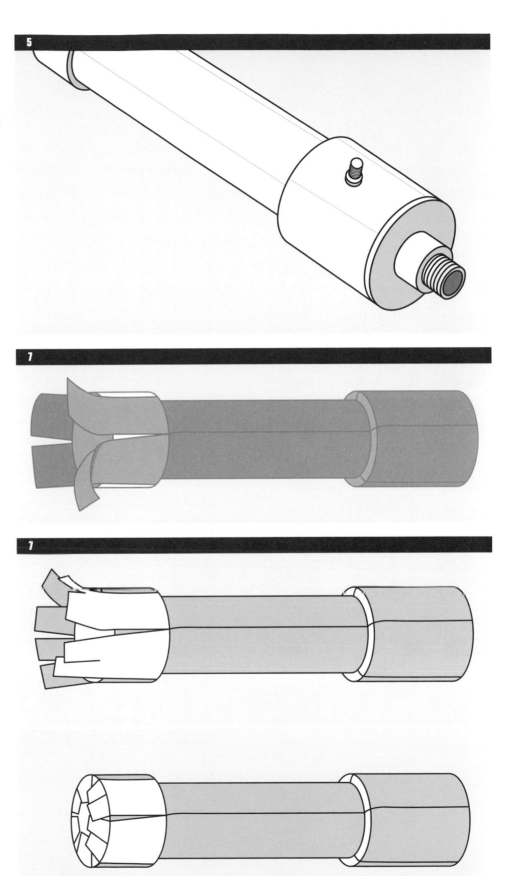

**8** To make the launch barrel and handle, cut two 1¾" (4.5 cm) pieces, one 6" (15 cm) piece, and one 24" (61 cm) piece of ½" (1.3 cm) PVC pipe. Arrange these pieces, the flexible PVC coupling, and the ½" (1.3 cm) fittings, as shown.

**9** Glue the pieces together. Spray paint the PVC pipe and fittings and wrap the flexible PVC coupling in decorative tape, if desired.

**10** Identify the direction of the airflow on the sprinkler valve. Most models indicate this with embossed arrows on the valve openings. Wrap thread seal tape around the threads of the pressure chamber and then screw it onto the sprinkler valve. **Make sure the arrows on the sprinkler valve are pointing away from the pressure chamber.** Tighten it until it's difficult to turn and the valve stem is pointing downward, as shown.

**11** Wrap more thread seal tape around the second ½" to ¾" (1.3 to 2 cm) PVC thread reducer and then screw it tightly onto the sprinkler valve.

Spray paint the threaded reducer before attaching it, if desired.

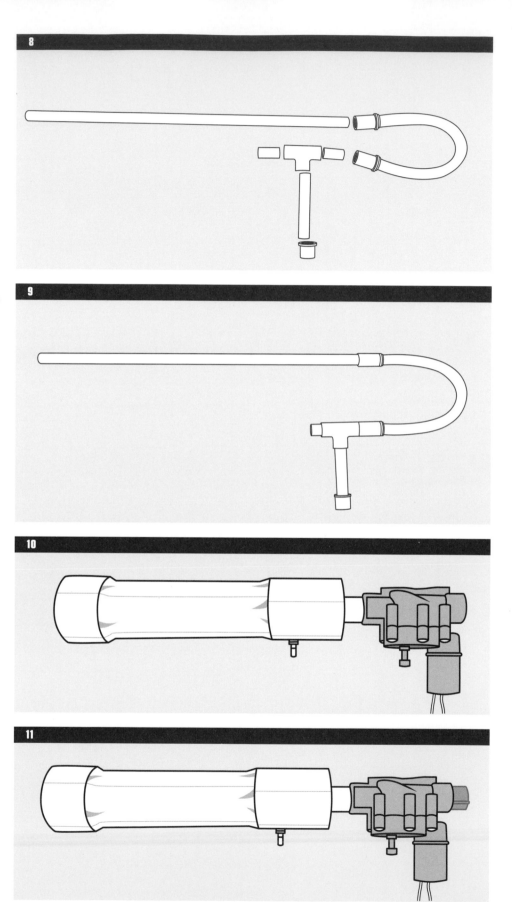

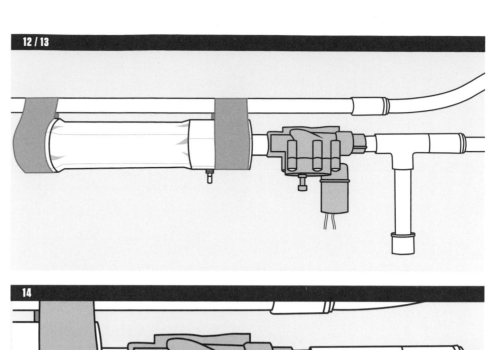

**12** Glue the launch barrel assembly into the threaded reducer, as shown. Make sure the handle, sprinkler solenoid (the cylindrical part that's connected to the wires), and valve stem all point in the same direction.

**13** Strap the launch barrel to the pressure chamber with heavy-duty duct tape in two places, as shown. You will need to bend the flexible PVC tubing significantly, which may be easier to do with a friend; have one person hold the pipe in place while the other tapes it down.

**14** Strip about 1" (2.5 cm) of insulation off the ends of the wires from the sprinkler solenoid, battery connector, and button. Tightly twist the exposed wires together, as shown.

Clip on the 9V battery and give the button a push. You should hear a small clicking noise coming from the solenoid.

**15** Wrap the exposed wire connections in tape to insulate them. Tape the battery onto the launcher and hot glue the button onto the handle. Tidy up the wiring by taping it against the launcher, as needed.

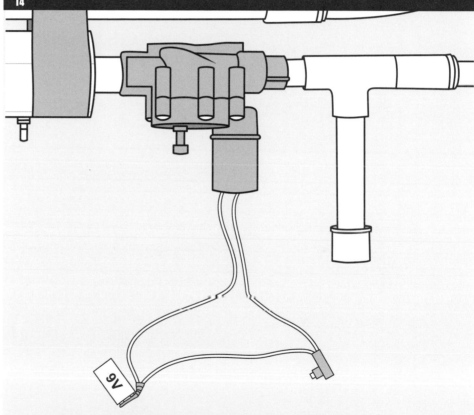

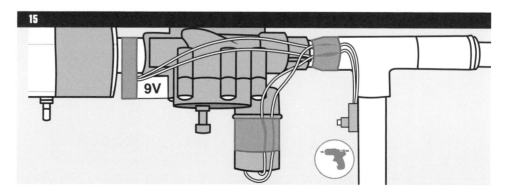

**16** Attach the pump to the valve stem and then tightly wrap the front of the pump to the front of the pressure chamber.

**17** Cut two ¼" (6 mm) pieces of ½" (1.3 mm) PVC pipe and fit them snugly between the launch barrel and the pump. This prevents the pump and barrel from bending when tape is applied in the next step.

**18** Tightly wrap another piece of duct tape to secure the pump in place. The rocket launcher is finished!

## SIGNAL THAT IT'S MADE FOR FUN

If you intend to use the rocket launcher outside where the public may see it, *wrap a noticeable amount of colorful tape around it, and paint the tip of the barrel red or orange.* This signals to others that your rocket launcher is not a real firearm.

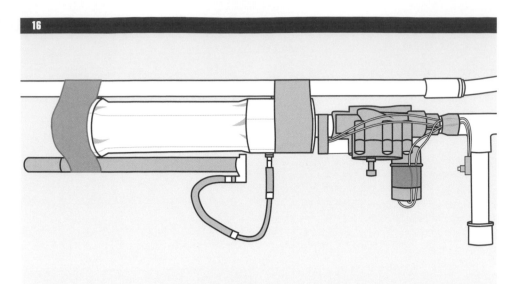

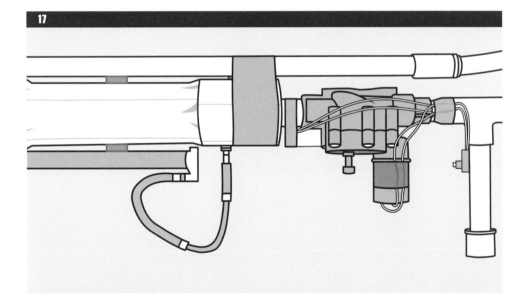

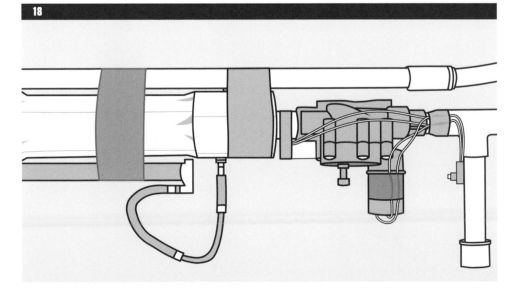

## MAKE THE ROCKET

**1** A rocket launcher is only as good as the rocket it's shooting. To make a superb duct tape rocket, center an 8" (20.5 cm) strip of tape along the short edge of a piece of the card stock so half of the tape is exposed, adhesive-side up. Center a scrap piece of ½" (1.3 cm) PVC pipe on the opposite end.

**2** Roll the paper around the pipe to form a tube. Hold the tube shape in place with the strip of tape at the end of the roll. Make sure you roll it firmly, but not so tight that it is difficult to extract the pipe from the paper tube.

**3** Make a nosecone for the rocket. Lay a roll of duct tape on the second piece of card stock and trace the hole in the center of the roll. Make a cut to the center of the circle.

**4** Overlap the edges of the cut until a cone forms and the bottom of the cone is the same diameter as the paper tube.

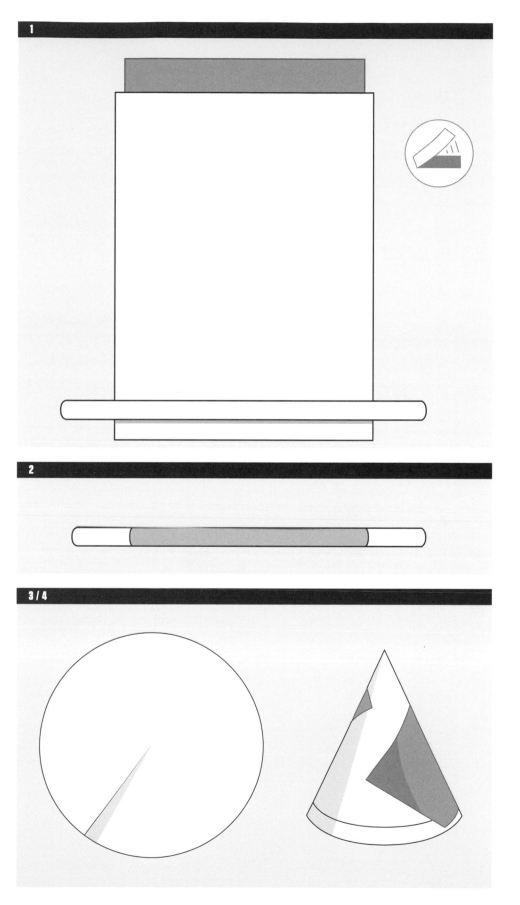

**5**_Cut several 4" (10 cm) strips of duct tape in half lengthwise. Attach the nose-cone by applying the tape strips length-wise along the rocket, as shown. Make sure the nosecone is entirely covered in tape so no air can escape.

**6**_Cut three triangular rocket fins from the card stock, each about 3" (7.5 cm) long.

**7**_Apply tape along the 3" (7.5 cm) side of one fin. Tape it into place at the base of the rocket, making sure it's parallel with the body of the rocket. Apply a second piece of tape along the opposite side of the fin so it stands out perpendicular to the rocket body. Repeat with the remaining fins, making sure they are all evenly spaced.

**8**_Cover any remaining exposed paper with a single layer of tape. This makes the rocket much more durable. Avoid applying too much tape, which adds unnecessary weight.

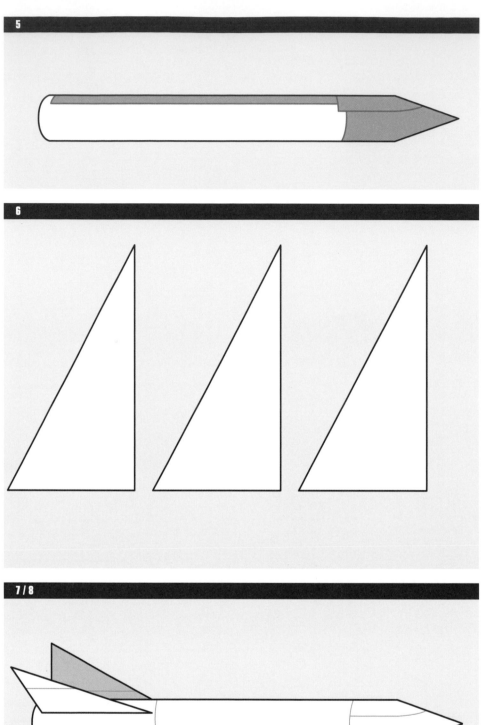

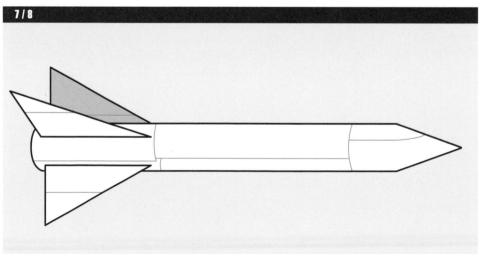

**9** Get ready to launch! Locate an open area, free of trees and rooftops.

**10** Begin pumping air into the launcher's pressure chamber. Stop when you feel resistance as you press on the pump handle. Avoid overpowering your first shot until you are familiar with the rocket launcher's power, or you may lose your rocket! If your pump has a pressure gauge, 15 PSI is sufficient.

**11** Load the rocket only after pressurizing the launcher. This helps prevent accidental rocket launches, which could cause serious injury.

**12** Take aim, strike a dramatic pose, and fire!

**TIP: STAY SAFE**

This project is safe to operate, but has the potential to be extremely dangerous. Avoid pressurizing the chamber above 50 PSI, and always aim upward to avoid accidentally firing directly at someone.

If you intend to take this project to a public area, check local and state laws to ensure that you are not at risk for a citation.

**BEYOND ROCKET LAUNCHING**
—

Tired of launching rockets? Sharpen the tip of the launch barrel with sandpaper and then stick a potato on the end, transforming the tuber into a projectile! (Remember to aim upward.) Try filling the barrel with water, confetti, or other harmless-yet-fun substances.

## MATERIAL SOURCES

**Duct tape**  Purchase online or at hardware stores. I recommend buying in bulk if you intend to make more than one or two of these projects. With duct tape, you generally get what you pay for, so avoid tape from dollar stores.

**Cardboard**  Shop around; cardboard box prices vary widely. Check moving companies or large hardware stores. Avoid buying from self-storage facilities or moving-truck rental stores.

**Clasps, straps, and buttons** Check fabric and craft stores.

**PVC**  Shop hardware stores.

**Bamboo poles**  Purchase at hardware or gardening stores. You can also buy ½" (1.3 cm)-thick bamboo online.

**Rocket Launcher Project**  Electronic sprinkler valves can be bought at hardware stores. Shop online for electronics, or check local hobby stores or electronics parts stores.

**Recommended tools (see chapter 1, page 11)** Shop online or at hardware and craft stores.

## ACKNOWLEDGMENTS

A big thanks to everyone involved in the creation of this book: to my sister Kaile for the photography, to the lovely Ali for the illustrations, and to the whole Rockport team for making the book come together. And to the ShurTech® Company for sending me so, so much duct tape to work with.

## ABOUT THE AUTHOR

**Lance Akiyama** combines tinkering and education into a single aspiration—to create a better world by inspiring the next generation of innovators with exciting hands-on projects. He has created project-based learning tutorials on Instructables.com, started an after-school engineering service, and is currently employed as a STEM-based curriculum developer for Galileo Learning.

Lance spends his free time designing elaborate plans for advanced contraptions, keeping journals in cryptic backward writing, and attempting to fly by strapping paper wings to his arms and leaping from rooftops. He lives in the San Francisco Bay area.

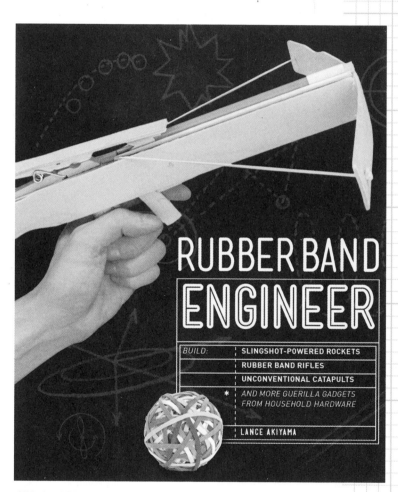

978-1-63159-104-4
Rubber Band Engineer

978-1-63159-016-0
Duct Tape

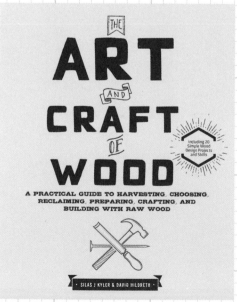

978-1-63159-297-3
The Art and Craft of Wood